The Residuary Legatee
The Memoirs of a Headmaster's Wife

The Residuary Legatee

The Memoirs of a Headmaster's Wife

Jean Glover

ISIS

LARGE PRINT

Oxford

First published in Great Britain 2003
by
Brewin Books Ltd

Published in Large Print 2005 by ISIS Publishing Ltd,
7 Centremead, Osney Mead, Oxford OX2 0ES
by arrangement with
Brewin Books Ltd

British Library Cataloguing in Publication Data
Glover, Jean, 1919–
    The residuary legatee : the memoirs of a
    headmaster's wife. – Large print ed.
    (Isis reminiscence series)
    1. Glover, Jean, 1919–
    2. Teachers' spouses – Great Britain – Biography
    3. Large type books
    I. Title
    371.1'0092

ISBN 0–7531–9310–8 (hb)
ISBN 0–7531–9311–6 (pb)

Printed and bound by Antony Rowe, Chippenham

Contents

Acknowledgements..................................vii

1. Background..1

2. Who goes there? 10

3. On your marks....................................27

4. Let battle commence 46

5. It never happens when I'm out 71

6. A welcoming environment 81

7. All comers...99

8. Public events 118

9. Greasepaint in the sherry................129

10. Out and about...................................142

11. Further out and about......................162

12. A safe pair of hands.........................187

13. Postscript 201

Acknowledgements

I would like to acknowledge my indebtedness to one of Her Majesty's Inspectors of Schools, who first pinpointed for me the true role of a headmaster's wife. "You will find," he said "that you are the fielder of all those jobs and problems which don't quite belong to anyone else."

Having found this to be profoundly true, I have called this piece of autobiography "The Residuary Legatee".

CHAPTER
ONE

Background

I was brought up between the wars in the gentle settled atmosphere of a cathedral city. Mine was in fact an uneventful childhood in a typical middle class family, going to the local excellent girls' high school for the whole of my education from kindergarten to sixth form, and then proceeding to university. Initially it has to be said that starting school, as I did, at the elderly age of six (I had apparently been "delicate") caused me problems, in that I had previously mixed with very few other children, as I indulged in what seemed an endless succession of childhood illnesses — measles of varying kinds, chickenpox, mumps etc. etc., but even worse no-one had thought to teach me how to read. The result was that, dumped into what seemed a howling mob of children I did not know, and then being told I could not sit with the few friends I did know — because I could not read — caused me considerable trauma, which I remember even now. My end-of-term report said it all: "Her tears are now less frequent." It also says a great deal for the careful handling of me by the kindergarten staff, that they had managed to restore the confidence of one who must have been a singularly

1

tiresome child. In fact by then two things had happened which contributed to my acceptance of the fact that, astonishingly, I found that school could be quite fun. The first was that I quickly learned to read. Catching what was apparently German measles for the third time, I was forced to stay away from school for three weeks, where someone thoughtfully provided me with a book called *I Want to Read*. I have never seen such a book again, but it must have been a remarkable one, as I certainly returned to school able to read and therefore able to take my place with friends of my own age-group. Though it has to be said that, though I could now read fluently, my writing — as in later years my husband constantly told me — bore all the hallmarks of someone who, however literate, was also someone who has NOT been taught to write. Certainly I had to admit it contrasted sharply with his own beautifully formed hand.

The second factor which contributed to my acceptance of school as a bearable, indeed quite enjoyable, place was that, now back in my own age-group, I could make proper friends. Like a lot of little girls I also found a "best friend" whose qualities of steadiness and humour helped to calm my still-present fears, mostly I think of making a fool of myself or doing the wrong thing. (It is nice to report that after more than seventy years we are still friends.) Somewhat to everyone's surprise it was found I could act and I was soon taking the lead in a number of little playlets, and the little bit of cachet I got from that also helped to boost my confidence. Many people seem surprised that a timid person can often act quite well on the stage. What they may not realise is that if you are acting, you are someone else, so no-one can hold you yourself responsible for anything that happens on the stage. At any rate I finally emerged into the main school a reasonably confident small girl, and made my way through it to the top with tolerable success.

All this time, naturally enough, I had no idea of what I wanted to do after I left school, and hopefully university. At one time I had great ideas that I would like to become a doctor, but my singular incompetence in mathematics put paid to that pipe dream. Then, like many girls who have some success in school plays, I had thoughts of becoming an actress. But my presbyterian father put paid to that one. "No daughter of mine will go on the stage," he said firmly — and meant it. Interestingly the thought that at one point in the future it might be quite rewarding to be a headmaster's wife did just cross my mind, though for rather irrational reasons. It so happened that my parents were friendly with the headmaster and his wife of the local grammar school, and so one afternoon I went with them to a play at the school and on afterwards to take tea in the headmaster's house. That tea party made a tremendous impression on me. I can visualise it now — the large lofty room with heavy furniture and maids flitting about dispensing cups of tea and delicious small cakes, and in the middle, behind the silver teapot, the resplendent figure of the headmaster's wife. I looked at her with admiration tinged with awe, and thought this reflected quite an enjoyable and interesting life. Interesting and enjoyable it certainly could be — but at that time I knew only one side of the picture.

On leaving school I went on to Oxford to read history which I enjoyed enormously, and made a great many friends of both sexes — despite the current thinking that if you have not been brought up with boys you will suffer a great disadvantage later, I certainly had no problem. My university years were stimulating and fun. I worked quite hard and enjoyed particularly the contact with much cleverer minds than mine; I went to the theatre nearly every week and after a time ran the college dramatic society; I played a certain number of games, if not with distinction at least with enjoyment, and, most important of all I joined the Bach Choir. Here not only did I thoroughly enjoy Monday nights all through my time at Oxford, but even more importantly, at my very first rehearsal I found myself sitting next to a very charming rather shy young man. He walked me home from rehearsal, and three years later I married him.

At the end of my first year at university the Second World War broke out. Initially it seemed that university work went on as usual for those already up, particularly during the first months of the "phoney" war, but of course there was a different "feel" to it. A proportion of men who had been in their first or second year did not come back, as they felt they should join the Forces, and as 1940 went on, the feeling of unease grew, and one wondered just what the future would hold for us all. I have a very vivid memory of listening to Churchill

4

speaking on the radio at the time of the evacuation from Dunkirk, and thinking seriously, perhaps for the first time, of what might happen to me if the Germans did come. Another vivid and very unhappy memory is of someone telling me that a friend with whom I had been lunching and swimming in a carefree way only the week before had been shot down over Kent. I had been due to see him again the next week. But we were young and we were resilient and most of the time we simply kept on working at our courses and enjoying the friends we had. Meanwhile the shy young man from the Bach Choir, who had gone straight into the army in September 1939 — he had done his finals the previous June — continued to come and see me whenever he had leave. At the beginning of my third year we got engaged, and two weeks after my finals we got married. Neither of us had any money of course — if I remember rightly he had an overdraft and I certainly had a loan to repay to the Bertha Johnson Loan Fund. But that seemed the least of our worries. None of us knew at that moment just what the future might bring, and it was a question of *carpe diem.*

The next four years we lived a curious existence like so many of our contemporaries. I remember how cross Robert used to get with me when I spoke in my no doubt carrying voice of a time when "we shall be properly married" (someone will hear!), but it certainly was not marriage as I had envisaged it when I was young. Robert was constantly moving with his unit to different places in England and Ireland and eventually abroad, and I got a job as a junior history teacher at

Alcester Grammar School — which I much enjoyed. When it was possible I tried to join Robert for a weekend, which often entailed quite a journey — I remember vividly arriving at Carlisle Station at 1 a.m. and having a moment of panic as there appeared to be no-one on the platform, until I suddenly caught sight of a pair of familiar feet on the table of the waiting room — Robert had not heard the train come in. And of course whenever he got a 48-hour leave he would come and see me. I shared a flat and later a tiny house with another member of staff, who was also married to someone in the forces, and we had a splendid arrangement that if one husband came on leave the other wife would disappear. But it was all an odd existence of ecstatic greetings followed only too soon by tremulous goodbyes.

After three years I moved on to be head of the history department at Lowestoft Grammar School — in a sentimental way I felt nearer to Robert, who was by now in Germany, if I was on the Suffolk coast. It was hard work — I had only three free periods each week, I remember, and taught the whole school from second to sixth form. But I much enjoyed it, though classes were large — I had 41 in my GCSE class, which tended to increase from week to week as children came back from schools to which they had been evacuated. They were also a very exuberant lot and I was warned particularly of one particular class of over 40. However, fortunately I established who was boss early in our relationship — and indeed earned myself the nickname of "Pistol-Packing-Momma" — and after that we got on fine. I am not sure they would have believed me if I had told them I had once had a school report that said, "Her tears are now less frequent."

At last, at the end of 1945, came the great change. Robert was demobbed, and suddenly I ceased to be a busy hard-working teacher, and became a little housewife in a Yorkshire village, "properly married" at last.

As Robert had gone straight from university to the army, he had no career to return to, and had had to think what he might do. One day, as we were discussing this, he said modestly, "I find that I enjoy teaching soldiers to do things, and I have noticed soldiers do what I tell them — I wonder if I should try schoolmastering?" And so it started. As he began to apply for jobs, he was offered several, for he had a lot to give to the profession. But what finally made him accept a post at Ampleforth — for we were not Roman Catholics — was that when he asked Father Paul the question he had asked all the other heads: "Where should we be able to live?", Father Paul replied, "We bought a little house in Helmsley the other day — you could have that." That clinched it — we had never had a real home, and so began four and a half happy peaceful years. While Robert learned and much enjoyed the art of schoolmastering, I had two little girls and learned to keep house and cook. Gone were the days, I am glad to say, when I cooked poultry without making sure I had taken out the giblets. Now I worked my way steadily through my new cookbook. Some things were more successful than others but Robert was astonishingly patient.

We were both aware however that this particular period of peaceful existence could not last for ever. We were not Catholics, and knew very well that in a Roman Catholic school there was no possibility of Robert becoming a housemaster, or even probably a head of department, and sooner or later he would want a fresh challenge. So after four years he began to look about for a post of more responsibility, and was very pleased to be offered the post of head of classics at Kings School, Canterbury, under the redoubtable Fred Shirley, a good school in a lovely city. Here we certainly settled very happily. Robert enjoyed his wider responsibility and teaching, and his rugger coaching, and I had another baby, a small boy, and found quite a niche for myself in the local dramatic society, and we imagined we would remain in Canterbury for a good many years.

However, after only two years, Robert came home one lunch time with a pleased look on his face. "Fred has been telling me that he thinks I have the makings of a good headmaster and I ought to start looking about me for possible posts," he said. I was of course delighted but not surprised, as I had by now realised that, not only was he a very good teacher but, with his genuine interest in the boys he taught, his unflappability, his steadiness and his great gift for organisation, he had in fact got those qualities so important in a head. "Splendid," I said. "I shall go into town at once and get a copy of the *Times Educational Supplement*." And so our horizons expanded. At that point, needless to say, I was not yet thinking of what qualities a headmaster's wife might need. That awakening came later. All I could really claim to offer that might be useful was four years' experience of dealing very happily with teenagers and a determination to "have a go".

CHAPTER
TWO

Who goes there?

For some weeks no-one showed any interest in Robert's occasional applications. Then one cold January morning an official-looking envelope addressed to him arrived by the second post. The day had started inauspiciously as Robert — who rarely succumbed to illness — and our second daughter, Jane, were both in bed getting over a bout of flu. Further, the baby was grizzly with a cold, and as a result of all this I was behind with the chores. However, as soon as I had sent Kate upstairs with the letter for her father miraculously all was suddenly changed. I heard an exclamation of pleasurable surprise followed by an imperious summons from Robert: "Come and look at this." "This" turned out to be a letter from the Haberdashers' Company asking him to come for an interview the following week in connection with the headship of Adams Grammar School, Newport in Shropshire and I was to go too. Immediately everyone felt better. Suddenly both invalids declared their intention of getting up, and an atlas was found so that we could pinpoint exactly where Newport was. All sorts of speculations were indulged in and plans made as to how we could get away for the night, as we had no living-in help, and, very important, what should we wear? At the same time I remember thinking idiotically that if this came off I would have to get a silver teapot. Memories of that splendid occasion in the headmaster's house in Lincoln came rushing back.

The problem of someone to leave the children with was soon settled — our trusty baby-sitter, the wife of a local verger, said she would be happy to sleep in and take charge. More difficult was the question of what to wear. Finally we decided that Robert's best suit, hastily cleaned, was quite acceptable, but for some reason he insisted in investing in a black homburg hat, which he felt would give him "tone". Even to my affectionate eyes he looked a little odd in it, especially as he never wore hats — and as far as I know he never wore it again after this occasion except for the occasional chilly funeral. But he was quite adamant that this was part of the correct equipment for an interview.

My clothes presented more of a problem, because for the last five years the only new ones I had bought were maternity clothes which we did not think looked quite suitable. A large outlay was, for obvious reasons, out of the question, but fortunately the January sales were just starting. So, next morning I bicycled into Canterbury and emerged an hour later with what I was convinced was "just the thing" at the astonishing bargain price — even for those days — of three pounds. It was an elegant little suit, and from its original price-tag a genuine bargain — so I ignored the fact that the narrow skirt made it rather difficult to walk in and the jacket was difficult to do up. Indeed I convinced myself that as long as I took short steps and stood about with the jacket carelessly thrown open it really did do something towards helping me acquire something of the sophisticated elegance I felt every headmaster's wife should have. "Shropshire," I thought "here I come."

The day for departure came at last. We were to travel up one day, spend a night in a small local hotel, into which we had been booked, and then, hopefully fully rested, Robert was to be interviewed next morning, while I, presumably with the other wives, stood around looking "suitable". So, after breakfast, once I had washed the Farex out of my newly-washed hair where my small son had liberally applied it, we set out for the station, I in my new suit, remembering to take short steps, Robert magnificent in "the hat".

I recall that train journey with enormous pleasure. It was one of those marvellous slow trains, complete with restaurant car — now long taken off — which meandered gently from the south coast to the midlands stopping at all kinds of unlikely places. And I had to admit it was most pleasurably peaceful to be able to enjoy the journey without small bodies, dearly as I loved them, clambering all over me, needing to be amused or comforted or fed. So I leant luxuriously back in my corner and watched the winter landscape go by. We left the orchards of Kent behind us, skirted London, and crossing the Thames, climbed into the Chilterns and then headed towards the Cotswolds. It was a beautiful clear day, and the bare trees stood out in their stark beauty against the pale blue of the sky. I

12

looked at the bare fields and marvelled as I always do, how the colour of the earth changes as you cross England, taking in an infinite variety of browns and reds. After a while we went along to the restaurant car to have coffee and later lunch. It was all very peaceful with a sense of "holiday". When, just once, I had said idiotically, "Do you think the children are all right?", Robert had replied with all the firmness and conviction of the born schoolmaster, "They are absolutely splendid, now just enjoy your holiday" — and promptly immersed himself in his book, emerging for a moment a few minutes later to say with a beatific smile, "I ought to be teaching 3B now — I wonder what lucky chap has got them."

Completely carefree enjoyment of a day out perhaps stopped with our arrival at Wellington station from where we were to catch a bus which would take us the last ten miles to Newport. Frankly it was not a comfortable ride. It was market day and I shared a seat with a farmer's wife of ample proportions who had apparently been buying more sharp-edged objects than you would have believed possible. I have often wondered idly what they could have been. Meanwhile Robert, looking resplendently incongruous in his Homburg hat, and delightfully unaware of this fact, had to stand all the way.

However he was obviously greatly enjoying a lively conversation with a farmer on the subject of crops, for though I was aware he knew very little on the subject he was one of those people who can always use what facts they have to their best advantage, and had a

genuine interest in anything to do with the country —
combined with the schoolmaster's knack of getting the
other chap to talk. The discussion was obviously being
greatly enjoyed by both parties.

As I watched him with affection, I was suddenly
seized by the fact that if we were on this bus, other
candidates might also be on it, and I began to examine
covertly the other occupants for "possibles". There was
a tall out-of-doors type man in a good tweed jacket —
could he perhaps be an ex-rugby-international after the
job? But he suddenly turned to the man beside him and
asked, "What's your fancy for the two-thirty tomorrow?
The going should be altogether too soft for Danny
Boy." Unlikely, I felt, that any candidate would be at
this moment concentrating on the two-thirty tomorrow.
Then there was the quiet scholarly-looking man — a
first in Classics perhaps? — but, rather to my relief he
left the bus at the third stop. My only other possible
candidate was a tall dark man in his late thirties whose
eyes seemed to be riveted in anxious amazement on
Robert's hat. He did not seem to have a wife with, him
— perhaps he was a bachelor, but at any rate he looked
nice, so I thought if he was one of us he would be
pleasant company.

At last the bus stopped in the broad main street of
Newport outside a small unpretentious hotel where we
were to stay, and as we advanced towards the door I
became aware that the man who had seemed to be so
fascinated by Robert's hat was also making his way
there. As we neared the door, my husband turned
round and said, "My name is Robert Glover and I am a

candidate for the headmastership of the school here. Would I be right in thinking you are another?" The man smiled and held out his hand. "Yes indeed," he said, "and I had already guessed you were one from the hat — most impressive." So, having shaken hands we entered the lounge of the hotel, and immediately found ourselves caught in a barrage of interested glances from nine pairs of eyes, five male, four female. The other candidates had arrived. We were the last.

Introductions were effected, none of which I have to admit I really took in — I was too busy studying what I thought was the strength of the opposition. The fussy little man, apparently already a head of another school, who rapidly made us all aware that he owned a car — very unusual for a penniless assistant master in those days — I brashly thought was not too much to worry about. But the tall well-built man who had an air of quiet authority, a pleasant sense of humour and a good handshake was, I felt, opposition number one. The other couples I admit I did not immediately register particularly, though a quick glance at the wives' outfits assured me that my £3 suit would compare perfectly well — provided I did not try to do up the jacket.

We retired to our bedroom to unpack and sank on the bed to take stock. "I think they mostly look pretty impressive," said Robert gloomily, "particularly that tall man."

"No more than you," I said firmly — and meant it. "Let's go and take a look at the town and see if we can get an unobtrusive look at the school." So once more we ran the gauntlet of appraising eyes as we crossed the hotel lounge, and then we were out again in the now-darkening street.

It did not take long to view the town, which consisted mainly, from our point of view, of the one broad street in which three banks, a small Woolworths and an even smaller Boots were sandwiched among a motley collection of little shops and a multiplicity of pubs. But near the bottom of the street the buildings suddenly became more interesting, for not only was there a handsome if somewhat dilapidated town hall, and a pleasant-looking church standing in a well-kept church-yard, but we suddenly came upon the school, as handsome a building as you would find anywhere. A width of decent iron railings separated the grounds from the road, with a handsome pair of iron gates in the centre. On each side of these was a small neat almshouse, each with its own tiny garden, and through the gates a flagstone path, flanked by lawns, led up to the splendid 17th-century façade of the original school building, before additions were made later. On the left as you looked at it was the original headmaster's house, still used as such, and to balance it on the other side was a similar building, originally the usher's house, but now given over to other school uses. In between was a cloister, now glassed in, and used as the boarders' dining-room, and above this, as we later discovered was a library, behind which was a beautiful panelled hall where originally all the teaching had taken place. The whole effect was most pleasing, and suddenly we both wanted to come here very much indeed. "Yes," said

16

Robert, typically laconic, "This would do. Now let's go and have some dinner."

On our way back to the pub something else caught our eye. A slightly decrepit but nevertheless functional cinema was showing Gary Cooper in *High Noon*. We immediately agreed that this was the very thing for this evening, much more relaxing than exchanging slightly taut pleasantries with the other candidates. Thus resolved we prepared to eat a hearty dinner.

When we returned to the pub however we discovered that there had been other suggestions for our evening plans. Apparently while we had been out the clerk to the governors had called in to offer us all an open invitation to attend a concert in the school hall that evening, given, I have to say, by a not-very-well-known trio with a frankly rather boring programme. Opinion was sharply divided as to what should be our right course of action. The fussy little man fluted on about how kind of the powers that be to provide us with entertainment for the evening, but others were not so sure.

Personally it was not how I wanted to spend this lovely unencumbered evening; I could think of few things I would dislike more than having to sit on a no doubt hard school chair, listening to this, to me at any rate, uninteresting programme, with the entire audience no doubt staring at us and no doubt making bets. Daring but desperate I said in a small voice in a pause in the conversation, "I am afraid I would much rather go to *High Noon* at the cinema next door." In the end we divided. Our original friend from the bus and the tall impressive man I had originally noticed elected to go to the cinema, and feeling rather like naughty schoolchildren had a merry evening with Gary Cooper and bought each other chocolate and ices. The others looking pious, though I thought some of them looked decidedly wistful, went dutifully to the concert.

We were both quite convinced we should not sleep a wink that night but in fact, with the insensitiveness of youth we both slept like logs and awoke refreshed and pleasantly excited. Breakfast was not an easy meal as with the men in their dark suits and the women in their "best" we all made slightly stilted over-jolly conversation. And I was certainly haunted by the fear of spilling egg or marmalade down my new suit. No-one was very hungry. As soon as it was over we made our separate ways, singly or in pairs, over to the school. Battle was about to commence.

I can still recall my feelings of excitement as we pushed open those handsome iron gates for the very first time. As we walked up the stone-flagged path, I remember thinking, "If by any chance we do get here, I shall border this path with crocuses in the spring and alyssum and lobelia in the summer." And then we were at the front door.

We were the last to arrive — I had had trouble with my hair which when newly washed always tends to shed its pins. The others were all standing rather self-consciously in a large tiled hall, while an elderly man in a gown, who turned out to be the second master, stood a little to one side waiting for us all to arrive, so that he could announce the order of battle.

18

The men were then given specific times for their interviews with the governors — Robert was to bat last — while the women were to be shown round the house, and then left to their own devices until lunch, which was to be held in the boarders' dining-hall. They would then rejoin the main party, and meet the governors, and presumably be looked over to see if they could represent a hazard as headmasters' wives.

We started our tour of the house being bear-led by an imposing, rather chilly, lady who was acting as a housekeeper and caterer. The previous headmaster had left the school a term before, at very short notice, to take up an exciting post abroad so while there was an interregnum this lady was doing the duties of catering and entertaining normally done by the headmaster's wife. The house was certainly very imposing with a magnificent oak staircase, but as it had not been occupied for some time, except by the housekeeper, it felt somewhat chilly and unlived in, and one got the impression of a succession of lofty rooms, filled with what seemed to be an excessive amount of antique furniture, rather than a family house.

The ground floor seemed to be a succession of halls, all flagged or tiled and rather cold, but at least there would be no problem of where to keep the pram. Then there was a smallish room, which appeared to have been used as a study, and, the *pièce de résistance*, a truly magnificent panelled dining-room, complete with a set of very handsome but exceedingly hard dining-chairs, dating from the 17th century, when the school was founded.

19

We then followed the austere housekeeper up the shallow steps of a very fine oak staircase to a broad oak landing. While I admired it, I remember wondering thoughtfully who polished all that oak. From here there led off two lofty bedrooms, each with its own solid-looking washbasin. What luxury I thought to have a washbasin in the bedroom, but perhaps "solid" was the right word, for as long as I knew them, nothing would go down those plug holes in under an hour. There was also a small, rather disappointing, bathroom but, to make up for it, a truly charming drawing-room with long windows, overlooking a walled garden. Instantly my daydreams of pouring tea out of a silver teapot came unbidden to my mind, though even then the practical side of me looking at the coal fire burning brightly in the grate could not help wondering who brought up the coal.

Another flight of those magnificent oak stairs led to another whole series of rooms, not so grand, but still spacious and lofty. Three large bedrooms led off from the lino-covered landing, while three other doors revealed a loo of memorable antiquity, a small staircase leading to a further tiny bedroom with a dormer window, and yet another small staircase which led to a cavernous room containing an ancient bath and, in the far corner, a minute, positively Victorian, gas-stove. From top to bottom I had counted 46 stairs — not a house for the arthritic.

"Well," said our bear-leader, "that is all." By this time the whole party was looking a little stunned, no doubt visualising, as I certainly was, what our own little bits

20

and pieces would look like in those enormous rooms. Indeed as we descended the stairs again, one of the wives said to me with a giggle, "I think all my furniture would go into just one of those rooms."

Punch-drunk though I was after our peregrination of room after room, I still had a feeling that there was something missing from this house — of course, a kitchen. Walking as fast as my tight skirt would allow me, I drew level with our formidable guide and asked simply, "Where is the kitchen?" She regarded me with condescending iciness. "Your meals, Madam, will of course be brought through from the school kitchen." "But what about the holidays?" I pursued. The supercilious eyebrows rose another fraction. "Will you be here in the holidays, Madam?" I wondered where else I would be, not being the sort of family who had property elsewhere. However with my last remnants of courage I persisted, "Where actually is the school kitchen?" She waved a languid hand. "Along that corridor — not really very far." We all looked down the corridor stretching into the distance. "It would be like cooking in the house next door but one," I murmured to myself, and again the wives immediately by me giggled. Eyeing us disapprovingly our mentor led us back to the drawing room where we were given coffee — very welcome if rather cold. But, as we agreed between ourselves, it had come a long way.

After coffee the wives were free to do as they liked for a while, and after a quick word with Robert, now waiting his turn to "go in" and looking remarkably calm sitting doing the crossword, I made a quick foray into

21

the little town. By day it was unremarkable but pleasant, and the shopkeepers I met were unhurried and friendly, and I wondered whether I should ever see any of them again. Meanwhile I bought chocolate for my homeward journey and two tiny china figures for my small daughters who had both started collections on their bedroom mantlepieces. I then returned to the school and was almost immediately ushered once more into the drawing-room where all the candidates and their wives were now assembled for pre-lunch drinks.

My first impression of the governors was that they were a very imposing body of men, and indeed particularly among the Haberdasher Deputation there were some distinguished men. The school I learned had been founded in the 17th century by a member of the Haberdashers' Company, one of the great twelve most distinguished companies, and they still continued to be responsible for the fabric of the school (though it now had voluntary aided status), and indeed their representatives comprised nearly half of the governing body. So there were present a well-known banker, a distinguished barrister and an ex-Lord Mayor of London, along with, more predictably, the local Bishop, a number of farmers, and various businessmen from the immediate neighbourhood, including, rather intriguingly, the local bookmaker. (I learned later that at some point a small committee had been formed consisting of a local magistrate and the bookie, but as, after it had been appointed, the bookmaker had a slight difference of opinion with the law, it never actually met, as it was felt, rather delightfully, to be rather embarrassing.)

I could see Robert on the far side of the room, perhaps a little more flushed than when I saw him last, and puffing rather determinedly at his pipe, but looking entirely cheerful and as I caught his eye, he winked. So far so good, I thought, and being at this point approached by the elderly barrister, proceeded to have a delightful chat about antique furniture, about which he obviously knew a great deal. Just before we were summoned to lunch we were all suddenly recalled to the stern reality of why we were actually there by the clerk to the governors asking for our attention and in pin-drop silence announcing that the governors would like to see Robert and two of the other candidates again after lunch, and everyone else was free to go. It was, frankly, rather insensitively done, and everyone tried to avoid catching the eyes of the obviously unsuccessful candidates, who melted away as soon as possible while the rest of us moved towards lunch. I was of course thrilled about Robert, but at the same time this second interview posed a problem. We were expecting to be able to catch the 4p.m. train from Wellington that afternoon, as it was the last one which would get us to Canterbury to relieve the babysitter who had made it clear she would only be able to stay the one night. As I stood pondering my problem, the old bishop approached me, asking genially, "What are you frowning about my dear? You ought to be cock-a-hoop, your young man is doing very well." Smiling gratefully, I explained the problem. "You go and catch your train, my dear," he replied firmly, "and leave your young man to follow — and keep your fingers crossed all the way

23

home. Meanwhile come into lunch with me and tell me about those tiresome children of yours. I bet they are not a patch on my grandchildren."

I enjoyed my lunch — the old bishop and a local university lecturer were delightful company, and the lunch was good. The whole occasion had a dream-like quality about it, and only once was I brought to earth with a bump, when a steely-eyed young man, whom I learned later was the very go-ahead young managing director of a local company, leaned across the table and said, "We should expect the headmaster's wife to cater for a boarding house of 80 boys and for all school functions. Would you be prepared to do this?" My heart gave a lurch. My degree was in history, and I had never in my life cooked for more than my husband and small children. However I managed to smile straight into his face and reply with apparent calmness (a little experience of acting on the stage can come in useful), "But of course," making the mental proviso "No doubt I can learn" — and learn I did.

Lunch came to an end, and after a quick word with Robert I went off to Wellington on my own in a taxi produced by the clerk to the governors. The journey home seemed interminable. My "whodunit" could not hold me at all. I kept wondering how the second interviews were going, and hoping that what Robert called my "artless prattle" had not put off any of the governors I had talked to. I had been very aware that at least one of the other wives had been voicing her views about education. I longed to talk to someone about it and, to distract myself, opened a conversation with the woman opposite me in the carriage. This was a mistake. She had recently been to hospital for an operation of unbelievable complexity, and I had let myself in for a blow-by-blow account of it followed by an equally exhaustive account of her sister's ill-health. However at length the train arrived at Canterbury and I hurried home through a drizzling evening. The baby-sitter was obviously in a great hurry to be off as she had apparently developed a splitting headache (I wondered a little guiltily what the children had been up to) so I had no chance of having a relaxing cup of tea with her.

I packed her off home, and rather apprehensively went upstairs into the children's rooms. I was relieved to see that perfect peace reigned. Coming downstairs, I wandered aimlessly from room to room, waiting for the phone to ring, turning the baby's nappies in front of the fire, giving the houseplants some totally unnecessary water. I had just put the kettle on to give myself a cup of tea to calm my nerves, when the phone finally rang. I rushed like a maniac into the dining-room where the phone was, idiotically not even waiting to put on the light but stumbling across the room by the light of a street-lamp outside and seized the phone. It was Robert. The jubilant "Hallo" told me what I wanted to know. "You had better start thinking of packing up," he said. "We shall be moving in April." Then after a brief resumé of his second interview — he too had been impressed by the razor-sharp young man who asked me about catering, and who sounded Robert on some of the problems encountered in school finance — he was

25

gone with a jocular, "See you tomorrow, headmaster's wife."

I sat quite still for a moment, the instrument still in my hand, and then suddenly and quite idiotically I did something I had not done for years. I did a handspring. Coming down somewhat heavily, I thought with amusement, "Good heavens, headmasters' wives don't behave like this", when suddenly I was aware of the room beginning to fill with steam: the kettle! I rushed into the kitchen to turn it off — almost empty but mercifully not quite — and returned to the dining-room to pick up things I had knocked over in my head-long flight, this time turning on the light. Having phoned my father — I simply had to tell someone — I made myself what tasted like the very best cup of tea I had ever drunk.

CHAPTER
THREE

On your marks

It was now mid-January, and we were to move in April. Eleven weeks seemed a very short time to prepare for a completely new way of life.

Robert of course had the greater challenge. He had a gift for teaching, and a wonderful way with the young. He had taught with great enjoyment for seven years and managed a department for two of them, but now he had to learn how to administer a school. He went up again to Newport the week after the interview to meet the masters and discuss timetables, and came back full of enthusiasm, but there were obviously problems to be overcome. With an absentee headmaster for the best part of last year, some things had obviously gone a bit at the edges, but, as he said, he had always fancied himself in the role of a new broom, and it just made the whole thing a tremendous challenge. A week later I too went up again, partly to measure for curtains and carpets, and partly to meet the domestic staff with whom I would be working. For somehow along the line the word "housekeeper" had been substituted for the word "caterer", and I was more than a little apprehensive as to what my duties would entail.

The second master, Mr Taylor met me at Wellington station and I thought then, and have never had any reason to change my mind, that he was one of the nicest men I have ever known. He had been a master at the school before Robert had even been born, and had acted as headmaster during the interregnum. But his loyalty to the new headmaster was unquestioning and generous, and he never indicated by so much as a look that the way he had been conducting things was the only or even the best way of doing things. I can recall him now, coming up the school path with a slightly rolling gait — the result of a football injury when he was a boy — dressed in a Harris tweed jacket and rather too short trousers, with his gown slightly askew, puffing at a short-stemmed pipe. He had a dry wit and a wonderful way with boys, of whom he had a great understanding and with whom he had a tremendous rapport, though he was always accusing them of being up to "some shenanigans" or "some skulduggery". He was a mathematician who also enjoyed taking the boys for carpentry as a Friday afternoon "option", and he was a devotee of the theatre and a good producer. In fact he was a good all-round schoolmaster who never had a moment's difficulty with discipline.

As we drove along, he filled me in with details of places we passed and people I would meet, along with a few gentle warnings of people with whom I must tread particularly carefully. I can hear him now: "Gently does it." I was so absorbed with what he was saying that the journey passed in a flash, and once more I was walking up that stone-flagged path, looking at the handsome façade of the school. But this time I walked straight into the house, my house, and up to one of the two lofty first-floor bedrooms, where I was to sleep.

That evening I dined for the first time in the oak-panelled dining-room, in the company of Mr Taylor — his wife was unfortunately not well and unable to join us — and the formidable housekeeper. I remember she was resplendent in a long skirt and made me feel very young and inadequate, still of course in my "interview" suit, as I had nothing else really respectable, and I was sure that she was only too aware it still would not do up with any comfort. The meal, a traditional roast, was well-cooked and served by a dumpy little woman with piggy eyes in a fat white face, and introduced to me as "part of our splendid husband-and-wife team of cooks". I smiled politely but took an instant dislike to her, and to the expression on her face which said only too clearly, "This one is easy meat."

We sat upon the handsome but extremely hard 17th-century chairs, and by the end of the meal I had formed a resolution to make cushions for those chairs as soon as I could afford them. The table was a beautiful old oak trestle one, and as I looked at it, I suddenly realised that our neat little mahogany dining-table would look ridiculous in here. Tentatively I asked, "This dining-table — does it belong to the previous headmaster?" The housekeeper replied at once, "Yes indeed, and I know it is one of the pieces he is willing to sell. I have a list here of what the local firm of auctioneers and valuers consider to be reasonable prices, and I understand you are to have first refusal." I glanced excitedly at the list, and my heart sank. Nothing, but nothing was within our range. This table for instance was listed at £65, no doubt a fair price, but no way could we afford it. As I looked up, I caught Mr Taylor's shrewd kindly eyes looking at me — I have no doubt he understood my problem.

"I have a better idea," he said. "Old Tom who helps me teach carpentry in the school is a really fine carpenter and I know he has some very nice pieces of seasoned oak. Suppose I bring him along in the morning to have a little chat with you. I am sure he would be only too pleased to make a table for you." I accepted the offer gratefully and in the morning Tom, a really splendid craftsman, came to see me and in time produced for us a very handsome oak refectory type table for the incredible sum of seven pounds and ten shillings, now valued in four figures.

Early next morning armed with notebook and foot-rule supplied by Robert and, hoping I looked efficient, I started to measure windows and floor space. It was not of course a question of how to fit things in — all we possessed would have fitted into that house many times. The problem was how to spread out what bits we had to make it at least look fairly furnished, and to make notes of what we would really have to acquire somehow or another. The question of floor-covering was partly solved by the fact that the house had fine polished floors, so did not need full covering, and though we only had a few carpets we did at least have some fine rugs, inherited from my father-in-law's college rooms, which spread tastefully if rather thinly about, would at least give the impression that someone lived there. But try as I would I became only too aware that, however I spread things out, and even if I made the children make do with the linoleum that was down in most of the top-floor rooms, we were still short of one carpet — until I had the bright idea that as no stair-carpet would be needed on those splendid polished stairs, we could sew up our present stair-carpet to make at least a partial covering for the child's room which had no linoleum. And this is in fact what we did. The carpet, when sewn up, still looked rather exiguous in the room, and indeed resembled nothing so much as a postage stamp put down rather crookedly on a large brown envelope, but our three-year-old daughter in whose room it was put down was always inordinately proud of being the owner of "the" carpet.

Measurements taken and sketch-maps made, it was now time for me to be introduced to the domestic staff.

We started in the kitchen. I had already met the wife of what the housekeeper had called "our splendid husband-and-wife team of cooks", and having taken an instant dislike to her, hoped for better things from her husband. I was disappointed. As I entered the old-fashioned kitchen in the company of the housekeeper who was to make the introductions, there were three people in it. The woman I had met last night was stirring something on a large Esse cooker; an elderly kitchenmaid was peeling potatoes in the sink, and in the corner, lying full-length on a tatty sofa, was a man doing the football pools. He eyed me insolently for a moment, and then, very slowly, got himself upright. We wished each other good morning, and then he said unpleasantly, "I understand you have no experience of catering — well you can leave all that to us." Alarm bells rang in my head, and I recalled the hint dropped by Mr Taylor in the car yesterday, that though the cooks cooked well, his wife certainly thought that from the bills they were also extraordinarily extravagant. However now was not the time for a confrontation. So, with the mental reservation "Not likely", I replied with simulated sweetness, "I am sure you will be a tremendous help to me", and passed on. I was however cheered by my meeting with the kitchenmaid, Mrs Whittle, a typical country woman who worked very hard, did not say a great deal, but no doubt missed very little of what went on.

We continued our royal progress. Next on the list was the school seamstress, a large somewhat asthmatic lady seated in a small building resembling the kind of ice-cream and confectionery kiosks one used to find on the promenades of seaside towns. Surrounded by the tools of her trade, and peering at me over piles of clean sheets, pillow cases, towels and underclothes, she irrelevantly reminded me of a latter-day Mrs Tiggy-Winkle. She looked at me benevolently over her glasses and wished me well.

There followed introductions to a succession of what the housekeeper referred to as "our dormitory ladies". They came in all sizes, tall, short, fat and thin, and my general impression was of cheerful country women getting on with the job in hand. Only one stood out as someone I felt I might have to be wary of. She looked at me with a calculating eye, and said in a not entirely friendly way, "All this is new to you no doubt." I was beginning to be able to cope with this one, and replied with careful ambiguity, "In this part of the world, yes." She had no idea what I meant, and I was happy for her to be in doubt.

The progress took some considerable time, as the dormitories were a long way from each other. Some were over Big School, in the original 17th-century block, while others were some way down the main street in houses taken over by the school from time to time and adapted to school use as the population of the school expanded. One of the houses, a handsome 19th-century building and originally the old rectory, also possessed a fine mature garden with extensive lawns, large herbaceous borders and a well-stocked vegetable garden. The house was used for junior boys, who were allowed to play around on the lawns and in the rough paddock beyond, while the vegetable garden supplied a good proportion of the vegetables needed for boarding masters' suppers and boarders' weekend lunches. From Monday to Friday they lunched with the rest of the school in the school canteen. The whole was looked after by a rugged character called George, a man of few words but a good gardener. Conversation was not easy, but gardening is a thing I enjoy, so I asked to be shown round. He threw a scornful look at my "best" shoes. "You'll get proper mucky in those," he observed. "However, the spring greens are worth looking at this year." He led the way in his large muddy boots, while I teetered after him in my town shoes, the heels of which kept sinking into the soft earth, so that wherever we stopped I had great difficulty in getting going again. However I plodded on and became genuinely enthusiastic about some really very fine crops. At one point we stopped by an apparently empty bed. "I suppose you will want to keep this?" he enquired lugubriously. "What is it?" I asked. "Sparrow Grass," he answered gloomily. "Silly stuff." I was thrilled, and said so. A mature bed of asparagus — what luxury. But George continued to be gloomy. "Don't do you no good," he observed. "A plate of turnips could beat it any time. And I suppose you shell your broad beans too?" he added suspiciously, as if this was the ultimate depth of culinary turpitude. "Well, Yes," I said in some surprise. "What do you do with yours?" "Boil 'em whole," was the reply. "You don't know what you are missing."

We finished our tour, and I prepared to take my leave. "Shall I send up what I've got on Fridays as usual?" he asked as a parting shot. I was surprised. How could I cater properly, I asked him, if I did not know what was likely to come? I would like to come down every week and see what there was and choose what I wanted, I told him. And anyway, I added with perfect truth, I enjoyed seeing how things were coming on. He snorted, but I don't think he was displeased. "Suit yourself," he said "but you had better wear more sensible shoes next time." We both looked at my poor muddy shoes. "You had better give me those," he added suddenly. "You can't go back to the old dragon like that." I thought it best to ignore his obvious reference to the housekeeper and sitting on a stool in the greenhouse, handed him my shoes. He made a very good job of them, with a pocket knife, some newspaper and a final rub from his scarf and I thanked him warmly. "Tuesdays and Fridays would be best," he added as we parted, rather like a doctor giving times of appointments to a patient — and Tuesdays and Fridays it was for the next six years. We had our arguments, particularly over the age he picked the runner beans — he liked to wait until they were large and fat and practically inedible — but he knew I genuinely admired his skills as a gardener, and within reason he would grow whatever flowers and vegetables I wanted. As a result my daydream of the stone path from the iron gates to my door being flanked first by a border of crocuses, followed by polyanthus and later alyssum and lobelia became a reality, and was greatly admired. Geraniums, to which he was devoted and I rather dislike because of the smell, might have caused a problem, but we came to a sort of compromise by which he grew them but only planted them a long way from the house, and so began a pretty harmonious association.

I re-joined the housekeeper who had stayed inside the boarding house. "What a time you have been," she commented as I rejoined her. "I find him a dreadful man and never see him unless I have to. I simply send down my order, and even then half the time he does not send it all." "Perhaps he has not got it," I suggested mildly. "He should have," she snapped. I could see relations between them had not been exactly cordial.

"Now for the laundry," continued my guide, "and that is highly unsatisfactory too. They never finish when they should and just blame it on the machines." I followed her to an outhouse in the garden which had been adapted into a small laundry, where two stout ladies were surrounded by a monumental pile of dirty washing. "It's them dratted ruggers again," said one of the women even as we opened the door. "Just look at them. They are bound to gum up the works." She held out a pair of extremely stained and muddy rugger shorts, looking rather like part of a commercial for a new brand of washing powder, except in this instance I could not imagine anything getting those shorts sparklingly white. I glanced at the two washing machines working away in the corner, and was suddenly appalled. They were not in fact industrial machines, geared to cope with those monumental piles in front of me, but ordinary domestic models built to deal with an ordinary family wash. But the lady holding the shorts was still in full spate. "We soak 'em as soon as we get here but the mud has hardened over the weekend and won't budge. So what can we do?" she wailed. "Couldn't the boys put them to soak in big tubs as soon as they take them off on Saturday?" I ventured. They looked at me in amazement as if the cat had spoken, and I realised neither of the laundry ladies had any idea who I was. At this point introductions were effected and I shook wet hands and we started on the problem again. "Soaking like that would help," conceded the other gentler lady, "but we haven't got big enough tubs." "And who would fill 'em and who would bring the ruggers down anyway?" The truculent lady flowed on. We beat the problem to and fro for twenty minutes. In the end my suggestion that a weekend soak might help was adopted, and the ladies were empowered to go to the local hardware shop to find suitable tubs. To an extent this did help this particular problem, but of course the whole concept of using domestic machines was ridiculous, for they constantly broke down under the unequal strain, causing crisis upon crisis. I got really quite fond of the two stalwarts, but I have to confess my heart used to sink every time I saw either of these excellent women advancing purposefully up the path to my front door. It spelled big trouble. In fact at this point in my life, I always maintained that if I had died and they had cut me open, they would have found the word BENDIX stamped across my heart. And when they finally broke down irretrievably and the governors decided not to replace them I felt as if a great burden had been lifted from me.

As we left the laundry the housekeeper glanced at me curiously. "Why did you take such trouble over those women?" she asked. "It was a problem for them to solve." I looked at her in amazement. "But they obviously did not know how to solve it," I said, "and who else could they turn to? This is not one to worry a headmaster with, and you tell me there is no bursar." She snorted, but I realised afterwards that it was at this point that I had really discovered the essence of my new job. I was the one they would turn to when there was nobody else obvious. I was in fact a "residuary legatee" of those problems for which no-one else was responsible.

But now I was to meet a very important person; matron. She happily turned out to be a charming efficient young woman, married to the art master, and they had rooms in the junior house. I was left to have coffee with her, and I felt at once that here was someone of whom I could ask questions without being snubbed or made to feel a fool. She gave me a quick résumé of how the boarding side was run, but she also provided me with a shock. After we had been talking for some time she looked at me curiously and said, "They did tell you, didn't they, that whenever I am off duty you have to stand in as matron?" I must have looked as appalled as I felt, because she added quickly, "It will be quite simple. You will find you merely have to cope with the odd bumps and grazes and dish out cough medicine. I shall supply you with everything you will need, and really nothing much ever happens when I am out." I was to remember those words a little wryly, but for the moment I was prepared to feel comforted.

The last "domestic" I met that morning was the young woman whose job it was to look after the headmaster's house. This was an unqualified success as we took to each other at once and all these years later we still exchange Christmas cards. She had been a children's nurse before her marriage, and was overjoyed to learn that I had three young children under five. "It will be lovely to have them running about," she exclaimed with genuine enthusiasm.

I left Newport that afternoon to return home, and in the train reviewed in my mind what I had seen and what I had been told, and tried to put a kaleidoscope of impressions into some sort of order. There were two major problems, I concluded to be faced; how to fit myself for the duties I was expected to undertake, and how to use the very limited money at our disposal to make the huge house appear furnished and resemble a home.

Robert listened to my catalogue of duties and said cheerfully, "Well, it is mostly common sense and you have plenty of that. You know what things can be grown; you are certainly used to washing dirty clothes, and you are not afraid of blood." "But the catering," I wailed, "How on earth do I find out what quantities are needed to feed around ninety people? I have never cooked for more than six." At this point Robert leapt up and walked across to a bookcase and produced a small paper-bound booklet entitled *The Manual of Military Catering.* "Try that," he said smugly, "I knew it would come in handy one day." I remembered the book well. When we were married I had been somewhat apprehensive about my lack of experience in cooking, and Robert, ever helpful, had produced this booklet which he had acquired when for a short time he had been a battery messing officer. At this point I had not been wildly enthusiastic about it, drawing his attention to the fact that all the recipes were for a hundred people and we were only two. I remember clearly his airy rejoinder: "Easy — divide by fifty." This still had not persuaded me to use the book, but now I grabbed at it as a lifeline and for the next four weeks kept it by my bedside, and drifted off to sleep murmuring, "30 pounds of potatoes, 20 pounds of cabbage."

As to the problems of furnishing, we sat down one evening and thrashed out the "musts". We studied the list of furniture left by the previous headmaster and decided sadly we could not afford any of it, except, we persuaded ourselves, the small television set. With the coronation coming up that summer, we simply could not resist the chance of seeing it in our own home.

With the previous headmaster's furniture not a possibility we then worked out how far our own furniture would spread. We obviously had beds, and I had noticed fitted cupboards in the main bedrooms. The dining-room had its beautiful chairs, and would soon have a table made by the school carpenter, but it was obvious we must acquire some kind of dresser. The large drawing-room we could just about furnish provided we could acquire a large sofa. But there were still what seemed like acres of halls and landings for which furniture must be found if the house was to look lived in, even when we had "dressed" them with the few bits and pieces we had. So I, as the sale-goer of the family, was sent off to acquire the largest pieces of passable furniture I could find for the smallest amount of money.

Over the sofa I was lucky. A local antique shop, whose owner had recently died, was to be sold lock, stock and barrel. There was a lot of publicity about it, and we were informed that London dealers were coming down to it. Even the catalogues were being sold at the then-unheard-of price of five shillings. Everyone told me I was crazy to even think of acquiring anything at such a sale, but I could not resist buying a catalogue and going along on viewing day. The sale was to start in the attic where presumably the less obviously attractive pieces or those in less good condition would be found. So I headed for there first and was rewarded with spotting exactly the sofa I wanted for our new drawing room. It was very large and very handsome, and it had been made in the early 19th-century. I knew at once it would "make" our drawing-room. So with the derisive comments of my friends — "You have not a chance" — ringing in my ears I duly turned up on time at the start of the sale. It was much less crowded than I had expected, and someone explained to me that the London train, bringing all the London dealers was late that morning, though it was expected any moment. I do not know if there is a saint in charge of transport, but he was certainly on my side that day.

The sale started on time at ten o'clock, and with a very long list of expensive antiques to get through that day, the auctioneer did not spend a great deal of time on the early lots. The first five went at what I thought were amazingly low prices, considering the importance of the sale, no doubt because the London train had still not arrived and many local bidders had presumably been scared away by the much publicised importance of the sale, thinking, as my friends had, that they would not have a chance. Lot 6 was "my" sofa, now lifted on high by two stalwart men. "This is an exceptionally fine early Victorian mahogany-frame sofa," read out the auctioneer in an expressionless voice, and to my pleasure someone behind me said quite audibly, "Certainly handsome: but too big for an ordinary room." "What am I bid?" continued the auctioneer, and I held my breath, quite sure that the bidding would even start way above my range. But to my relieved astonishment first there was silence then a tentative "five pounds" came from the back of the room. "Any advance, on five?" asked the auctioneer, and in what I hoped was an unenthusiastic take-it-or-leave-it sort of voice I squeaked, "Six." "Any advance on six?" asked the auctioneer. A moment's unbelievable silence and then: "Knocked down to the lady on the left for six pounds. Lot number 7 please."

I could hardly believe my luck. Lot number 7, a pretty antique "shield" mirror also went astonishingly cheaply but just as it was knocked down to some other lucky bidder there was a sudden surge of bodies in the doorway. The London train had arrived. The result of that was immediate for lot 8, another "shield" mirror and an absolute replica of lot 7, went for eight times as much as the first one had fetched and all other prices followed suit.

Once I was sure my trembling legs would carry me, I started to edge my way out of the saleroom to pay for my precious sofa and arrange for transport. As I waited by the cashier's desk, a grey-haired man approached me. "I understand you bought lot 6 for six pounds," he said. "It is not everybody's piece but it so happens that

I have a client who is looking for one like that to make up a pair. So I would be prepared to offer you sixty pounds for it, which would give you a nice little bit of profit, and probably enable you to buy something more suitable." He smiled ingratiatingly at me, and just for a moment I was tempted — sixty pounds was a lot of money. Then I thought if he was prepared to offer me — no doubt realising I was a thoroughly inexperienced bidder — sixty pounds, it was no doubt worth a good deal more. And, even more to the point, it was just what I wanted. So, smiling ingenuously at him, I explained, "I am so sorry but it happens to be the one thing I particularly wanted," and turned away.

That was our most spectacular bargain but we did have one less spectacular piece of luck. Looking round a Victorian house one day for any suitable bargains, I came upon a huge and astonishing piece of furniture in one of the upper rooms. It consisted of a tall chest of drawers flanked on each side by a full-length hanging cupboard — his-and-hers no doubt. The whole thing was surmounted by an impressive pediment and measured all of ten feet across, and indeed resembled nothing so much as the west end of a gothic cathedral. Other viewers seemed to pass it by exclaiming, "What a monster of a thing", but I observed both that it was beautifully made in solid mahogany, and, looking at it carefully, that it had been made originally in four separate parts — the two end cupboards, the chest of drawers and the pediment. Therefore I calculated it should not be beyond the skill of a competent joiner to separate the parts, and with a cunning use of a certain amount of mahogany veneer to make two smaller, acceptable pieces of furniture.

The sale started and, as it was not likely to be a supremely lucrative sale, went at a good pace, and soon got to the upstairs bedroom where I was lurking beside my "cathedral front". "Now what about a nice little piece of furniture which will take all those clothes the wife will buy —" started the auctioneer jovially. "No need to buy anything else if you buy this. Now who will give me a bid?" There was a certain amount of chaff about the size of the thing, and then swallowing a little nervously I said, "Five pounds." People turned round to see who had made this bid, and the lady behind me said in a kindly manner, "Are you sure you know what you are doing, my dear? It's very large you know." "Knocked down to the young lady for five pounds," said the auctioneer quickly, perhaps afraid I might change my mind. "A lovely piece of wood you've got there — you had better take up woodwork," he added encouragingly. He then led the gallery of potential buyers, tittering a little at my expense, on to the next room and I was left alone with my monstrosity. But for all the jesting it turned out to be a very good buy. My joiner friend, who fetched it away, confirmed that it came apart into four pieces with the greatest of ease. At a very reasonable price — for he took into consideration a considerable quantity of beautiful mahogany for himself from the pediment — he made for me two handsome pieces of furniture which I have to this day. The centre portion, once he had replaced the clumsy wooden knobs with brass handles suddenly became a very handsome tallboy, which looked splendid standing on one of the landings in our new house, and the two ends, joined together to become a very acceptable wardrobe.

Of course not all sales were like that. I recall long afternoons where I sat and watched one possibility after another go beyond my price. It was on one such afternoon I acquired a solid and useful, but not particularly attractive, oak stool — useful for "putting things on", known still to the family as "the furniture". For as I was going out that day my three-year-old daughter had asked me what I was going to buy, to which I had replied, "Furniture". So when I returned later clutching my one pathetic acquisition, my literal-minded daughter carolled happily "Mummy's got the furniture", and "the furniture" it has been ever since, which sometimes causes mild confusion among our guests when asked to put down a bag on "the furniture" by a member of the family.

So, with what furniture we could afford now acquired, new curtains laboriously made by me for the main rooms, and other curtains adapted in weird and wonderful ways for the other windows, by the time April arrived we were more or less ready — on our marks.

CHAPTER
FOUR

Let battle commence

The day for the move arrived. The two small girls had
been taken to stay with kindly aunts until the worst of
the upheaval was over, which made the packing-up
much easier. I was to travel up with the baby by train in
the morning, while Robert followed in the afternoon
when he had seen out the furniture. I had been rather
apprehensive about travelling all that way with an
eight-month-old baby who I was sure would become
fretful and bored, but I need not have been worried.
Richard quite obviously thoroughly enjoyed this new
experience, and when he was not sleeping contentedly
in his carrycot was already displaying all those skills in
industrial relations which he showed in later life by
getting on with everyone in the carriage, and the
journey actually passed merrily. Moreover I had with
me a young girl of sixteen who was coming with me to
be a nanny, as we had realised that with my
commitments in the school kitchen it was essential to
have someone we trusted to be with the children in the
nursery. I certainly felt very grand arriving with my own
"staff", however young.

Arriving at Wellington, we took a taxi to Newport where we were to stay the night at the same small hotel where we had stayed before the interview. Later that evening Robert arrived to confirm that our move out of the Canterbury house had gone without a hitch, and the removal men, already on their way, would start unloading at eight o'clock the following morning. And, true to their word, there they were at eight o'clock moving our furniture — what there was of it — quickly and expeditiously into our new rooms. At least, as they said, with rooms of that size they had plenty of room to manoeuvre. The house still looked a little under-furnished, but the new sofa, the two parts of the "cathedral" and other acquisitions looked splendid in their appropriate places. Richard's pram was unloaded from the lorry, and he was wheeled in triumph into his new home, where he established an instant rapport with Mrs Lock, the very nice person I had met who looked after the headmaster's house, and founded a basis of affection which has lasted until the present day.

As the men left the wife of the "husband-and-wife cooks team" arrived to see if she could help and insisted on helping me make up the beds. I have to admit I was rather reluctant to have her do this, as I was very conscious of the thin blankets inherited from my mother-in-law and the sheet mended sides to middle (it would be that week!) but perhaps she meant it kindly.

For the next few days we settled in, and with the arrival of our two small daughters and the sight of the pram in the hall and toys lying about it began to feel like home. During this time meals arrived from the school kitchen, and I had thought this would continue until the beginning of term, when on Friday lunchtime the cooks suddenly announced they were going off for a long weekend, as term was to start next week, and they gave me to understand that I should be extremely grateful to them for their splendid example of supererogation which had prompted them to cook for me over the last few days during our move into the house.

That weekend I learned the true meaning of the situation I had laughingly referred to at the interview as "cooking in the house next door but one", as I took over cooking for the family. The school kitchen was down a long passage, in the middle of which was a tiresome swing door, after which one had to negotiate a series of worn stone steps. The kitchen itself was vast and the pantries where one stored such things as meat, milk and vegetables were on the far side of it, seemingly another day's journey away. In fact to cook a simple meal involved an incalculable amount of leg-work. Washing-up took place in a scullery, also on the far side of the kitchen and, as the main hot water had been turned off until the beginning of term to save expense, had to be done with the aid of kettles boiled on the Esse stove in the main kitchen. As I struggled to and fro with laden trays, I have to admit I thought wistfully of the compact kitchen I had left in Canterbury. Nursery teas posed their own particular problem. It seemed sensible for the children to eat their high tea at the nursery table and I would cook whatever simple thing they had on the ancient stove in the cavernous top bathroom, but it seemed that whenever I was doing this the front door bell would go and that meant 46 stairs down and 46 stairs up again, as my knees well remember. However I survived that weekend with nothing worse than rather weary legs, well aware that the real first test of my ability to cope would begin next week when I had to demonstrate my catering skills — if any.

I had spent a lot of time studying past menus which the housekeeper, at my request, had left for me. I was thus able, with my constant companion the *Manual of Military Catering*, to draw up what I considered were workable menus for the coming week, and so work out what had to be ordered for them. The menus had to cover daily breakfasts, high teas and light suppers for the boys, and lunches for the family and kitchen staff and dinners in the evening for the resident masters. At the weekends I also had to cater for lunches for the boys and resident masters. When it came to do the ordering of supplies I was astonished to discover I had to start from scratch, as the vast store cupboards contained nothing, literally nothing, but a small tin of prawns. Where the residue of supplies from last term had gone to I could only surmise. All I was sure of was that presumably the present cooks did not like prawns.

The cooks seemed slightly surprised when I produced my menus and quibbled at one or two items, no doubt to put me in my place, I thought. But at least they accepted them, though making clear that they were definitely fourth-class menus. Nor could they find

49

much wrong with the quantities of goods I was ordering, though they looked with loathing at my catering manual which I clutched constantly. So I felt confident enough to go and place my order with the local shops which I was told supplied all the goods needed for catering for the school. It struck me that, particularly as the catering bills had seemed very high, this might be a rather extravagant way of proceeding, but at that point I was not yet secure enough in my new post to think of changing procedures.

The grocer turned out to be a particularly nice man and gave me very considerable help. I told him I thought I would have to "have a go" at reducing the school's bills, and wondered whether it would not be more economic to buy some things wholesale, and he very sensibly offered to negotiate some agreements for me with some manufacturers. As a result I bought goods at less than retail price, and he kept my custom, and if as a result I still paid a little more than I would if I had negotiated the agreements myself direct with the wholesalers, I kept the goodwill of a very useful ally, who would fight manufacturers for me over faulty goods, and further open up his shop at any time of day or night if I had a crisis. In view of my inexperience this seemed a wholly acceptable state of things. In fact he became quite a friend of the family and whenever the children accompanied me when I went to give my order on a Monday morning, before any school business was transacted, the three of them lined up at the cheese counter like three mice to receive their ceremonial piece of cheese, which he always gave them.

My first real crisis however occurred when my first order from the grocer was delivered. I had put all the groceries away in the appropriate cupboards with the help of the woman-cook, then put out onto the kitchen table everything that the cooks told me they would need for the next 24 hours and proceeded to lock the cupboards. It was at that point that all hell broke loose. The male cook who had, as usual, been reclining on the sofa rose suddenly and advanced threateningly upon me. "Don't you lock them cupboards," he announced, "for if you do, we'll walk out." I looked at him in amazement. "But I must lock them," I said. "You have everything you can possibly want for the next 24 hours, and all sorts of people walk through the kitchen. It simply is asking for trouble to leave them open." "If you lock them cupboards we walk out," he merely repeated, adding with more than a touch of malice, "and you don't know how to cook for ninety." We looked at each other. "Those cupboards are remaining locked," I said as firmly as I could, pressing my knees together so that he should not hear them knocking. "I will give you what you want when you want it, but it is simply neither safe nor sensible to leave stores open to all and sundry." "Right," he announced insolently, "then we are going and you can take our notice as of now." And with that he strode out of the kitchen followed by his wife.

Some of the boys, though thank goodness not all of them, were due back in an hour and a half, and would be expecting their high tea. I looked at the kitchenmaid, and trying to keep the tremor out of my voice said, I hope, brightly, "Well, it is only baked beans on toast for tea, and they will not all be in, so I am sure I can manage that, if you will help me, especially with things like how much tea goes into the tea-urn, and basically how long things take." She smiled, God bless her, and said at once, "Of course I will help. Once you know, there is really not all that to it. I am afraid I cannot get in until after breakfast in the morning but I will get here as soon as I can, and I will tell you how to go on with cooking the bacon and tomatoes and fried bread, and if we can get the trays of bacon prepared tonight, you should not have any trouble." So together we filled the urns for tea, and opened tins of beans, and made toast — no problem here — and in the intervals we cut the bacon and laid it on trays ready to be cooked for breakfast in the morning. Meanwhile I had put the meat in for the masters' supper, and Mrs Whittle had prepared vegetables, so that was in train, and I found to my relief that a cold dessert was already in the fridge. From time to time I rushed back into the house to make sure the children were all right, but our young nanny, Anne, was coping very well getting them their tea and putting them to bed, but as I returned to the kitchen I thought to myself, "What would I do without her?" Anne was not a luxury, at that moment she was a necessity.

After a while four of the younger boys came into the kitchen. I had been told that there was a rota of boys whose duty it was to help serve the meal, and then have their own meal afterwards. They looked at me with mild surprise and asked, "Where are the cooks?" "Oh, they had to go out unexpectedly," I replied airily, "so I shall have to rely on you to show me how it all goes." "Sure," they replied unquestioningly, and banged around, laying up tables and chatting cheerfully the while. A few minutes before tea was due to be served, one of the boarding-masters who was on duty that night appeared, and in his turn asked, "Where are the cooks? They have been seen going back to their flat. What is going on?" I saw no reason for hiding the truth from him, so I replied quite openly, "They have been extremely insolent and walked out because I insisted on locking the store-cupboards, which I did in accordance with my instructions from the governors." He looked at me with utter horror. "You can't upset them like that," he said. "What is going to happen to our dinner?" I could at this point have willingly hit him, but I restrained myself and said a little coldly and rather grandly, "That is under control. The headmaster and I would be very pleased if you and your other bachelor colleagues would dine with us tonight." There was really nothing else he could say at that point but "Thank you", which he did, and promptly beat a hasty retreat, though still looking none too pleased. "Difficult young man," remarked Mrs Whittle, looking after him. "They tell me he is very efficient but he thinks he is God. He has been in complete charge of the boarding side since the last headmaster left, and I suppose it has gone to his head. The cooks used to keep him sweet with giving him steaks. I dare say he won't like it if they are not here to fuss over him." My heart sank. I looked gloomily at the meat I was cooking and hoped it would please the young man. Mrs Whittle came over to me. "That meat will be fine, and I will make the gravy and get everything dished up before I go. It won't matter my catching a later bus just for one night." So I thanked her gratefully and went back into the house to prepare the table and get changed and prepare for what I could see would be the next "round".

It was not an easy meal that night. The meal itself was, thank goodness, perfectly all right — one can't normally do anything very dreadful to a grapefruit, and a good joint of meat, and the pudding left by the cooks, I had to admit reluctantly, was rather good. But the company could hardly have been called relaxed. There were just five of us present. Robert and I and the three young bachelor housemasters, one of whom I had already met. As time went on I realised he was really quite a nice young man, as well as being an efficient one, but he was not at his best that night, being obviously convinced that this awful new woman was going to undermine his comfort. Of the other two, one was a rather unattractive and undoubtedly lazy Australian who, astonishingly, appeared to be in charge of the English department. Listening to him I found myself wondering just how Shakespeare sounded in his classes. More importantly however, when Robert looked into it the English results at both GCSE and A-level were quite disgraceful. Not surprisingly he did not stay long with us after Robert discovered this. He did not like being persuaded to do some work. That evening we all talked of this and that, but there was no warmth or welcome in their attitude. Robert, as ever managed to appear perfectly relaxed, but I felt I must appear to be trying too hard.

However at last the meal came to an end and they prepared to go off to their separate houses. As they were going the young man I had met originally had one parting shot. Turning to me he asked stonily, "What happens about breakfast if the cooks have really taken umbrage?"

I had been expecting this so was able to answer apparently perfectly calmly, "I cook it of course." Robert eased the situation by putting a friendly arm round my shoulders and announcing cheerfully, "You don't have to worry — she is very efficient." Efficiency was the last thing I felt at that moment, but I tried to smile in what I hoped was both a modest and efficient way. The young man grunted and departed.

Breakfast was scheduled for 7.45, but I was down in the school kitchen by 6 o'clock, determined it should not be late. The bacon had to be cooked on trays in the oven, the fried bread fried in vast frying pans on top, and the tomatoes heated in a vast aluminium saucepan. When all was ready they had to be divided between six large dishes for the main tables, a smaller one for the boys who did the waiting to have afterwards, and then two other dishes prepared, one for the boarding masters, and one for my own family. None of it was really difficult — it just took time, and of course I soon discovered that if you turned your back for a moment the bacon got over-frizzled or the bread burnt. And on top of everything else coffee and toast had to be provided for the masters. But, with the help of the serving boys, who turned up 15 minutes before the meal and doled out marmalade into dishes for each table and reminded me how soon the tea should be made for it to infuse properly, everything was on the tables on time. I was just beginning to congratulate myself and prepare to take off my apron when one of the serving boys came out of the dining-room, looking very embarrassed and carrying the masters' toast-rack. "They say some bits of the toast are burnt," he mumbled. I could have wept. I was tired and hot and I wanted my own breakfast. However I managed to say, as evenly as I could, "What a shame — I'll do some more." I stood by the grill and watched that toast brown to exactly the right shade, and sent it back, wishing I could coat it with arsenic, then finally prepared to take off my apron. At this point Mrs Whittle arrived, and gave a quick glance round. "Got it on time did you?" she commented. "I knew you would." That was comforting, and, with a slightly lighter heart, I returned to my own house to be enveloped in my family's affection. "Well done," said Robert and, ever-practical, added, "This very morning you can go out and buy an electric toaster for the masters' use — and they can damned well do their own", while my kind elder daughter assured me, "It is the best bit of bacon and fried bread I have ever eaten."

Breakfast over, I firmly carried the baby upstairs to share the relaxing pleasure of his morning's play, while Anne manfully tackled the washing. At last, refreshed by the loving familiarity of family life, I metaphorically girded up my loins for the fray and returned to the school kitchen. As I entered I was surprised to see the two cooks, dressed in their kitchen aprons, standing there talking to Mrs Whittle, who was in the middle of saying with undeniable relish, "Oh yes, no problem with the breakfast and right on time." Then they saw me and there was a pregnant silence. "Good morning," I said, and waited. The man gave me an ingratiating leer. "It's like this," he said. "I think perhaps we were ALL a bit hasty last night." I didn't care for the "all". "Yes?" I said interrogatively. I wasn't going to help him. "It's a bit hard on you, being so new," he went on with a great show of magnanimity, "so we thought perhaps we would withdraw our notice, seeing as you can't really manage without us." The last half sentence was a mistake on his part. I had frankly been wavering at the thought of having even some sort of security in the kitchen until I was well and truly in the saddle, and I was very tired. But the taunt reminded me of their insolence last night and of those empty store cupboards and high bills. "Very well," I said. "Take it back for the moment and we will see how we get on during the next month. Now, what would you like out of the store cupboards for the next twenty-four hours before I lock them up again?" A look of pure malevolence replaced the ingratiating grin, but we both knew that at the moment they had nowhere else to go if they left, as they lived in a flat on the school premises.

The next two weeks were very strange, as we lived out our uneasy truce. I was perfectly aware they were applying for jobs, as they twice disappeared, presumably for interviews, in the middle of the day. They would certainly get something soon, I was equally certain, even without any reference from me as apparently the old housekeeper had given them a glowing one. Experienced cooks who could cope with numbers were like hen's teeth, few and far between, and they would undoubtedly find a ready market in hospitals, schools or similar institutions. I, on the other hand, as there was no definite arrangement for them to go, had my hands tied. I could not even advertise, I was told.

As long as they were there however I have to say they kept to their side of the bargain. They cooked all the meals efficiently, if silently, giving me no cause for further complaint. I spent a good deal of time in the kitchen at that point, not because I relished their company, but I knew I must see how they did things, so that I should have some idea of how to cope when the blow fell, as fall I knew it would.

The blow actually fell on a Wednesday morning, just after breakfast two weeks after the beginning of term. I had come through to the kitchen as usual to put out all that was needed for that day's menus and found them standing there in their outdoor clothes. The woman, with whom I had managed by now to establish some kind of rapport, was looking embarrassed but the man was looking satanically triumphant. "We are off," he announced. "Our new place just can't wait for us to start." Even though I had been expecting it I have to admit my heart sank to my boots. However I managed some sort of watery smile and held out my hand. "Goodbye," I said. "I hope you enjoy your new job."

His face dropped comically. He had obviously envisaged a scene of me begging them to work out their notice — as indeed they should have. However I was mindful at that point of my Scottish grandmother's advice to me on one occasion: "Never have a scene unless you are quite sure you can achieve something positive from it." And at this point I was sure the only result of having a scene would be to give some satisfaction to the cooks. But they had one more card to play. As he turned away the man said with an impudent sneer, "You haven't forgotten it is fish day have you?" Fish day. Eighty awful lumps of cod to be prised out of a wooden box delivered by the railway and fried for the boys' tea. It was one of their favourite teas, but not mine. However, "Of course, thank you for reminding me," I managed to say, as I plunged into the store cupboards.

I put out the day's provisions completely mechanically, and then, locking the store cupboards I did a thing I had never done before, nor have I done it since. I simply walked blindly out of the house, not really knowing where I was going. I "came to" in a field behind the school grounds staring at some cows and daisies. I stood there for nearly ten minutes before I finally managed to pull myself together, and saying aloud, rather to the surprise of the cows, "Come, this won't do", retraced my steps.

As I walked through the school grounds, lessons were changing and I was rather cheered to be greeted in a friendly fashion by a number of my boarders. Then entering my own garden I had an enthusiastic welcome from the baby, now in his pram. Finally, as I entered the house I was met my Mrs Lock, who had obviously heard the news and who said, with friendly concern, "I expect you could do with a cup of coffee; I'll fetch you some from the kitchen."

I drank the coffee and thus fortified returned to the school kitchen, where I found Mrs Whittle stolidly opening the box of fish which had just arrived, and counting out the pieces of slippery horror onto large trays. "I have been thinking," she said without preamble, "when you advertise, don't advertise for two cooks, or you will probably get a man-and-wife team again, and if one goes they both go. Advertise for a cook and a kitchenmaid." I thanked her warmly for what was obviously sound advice. But she was going on: "A cook and a kitchenmaid — that is really what you want. You don't need two cooks — he never did a hand's turn, you know, except to make fancy cakes — and you can't feed schoolboys on fancy cakes." She turned back to the fish but I had a feeling there was still something she had not said. "You don't happen to know anyone who might be able to come as a kitchenmaid?" I enquired hopefully. "Well," she paused again. "It so happens that when Doug the groundsman came in just now to pick up some cabbage leaves for his son's tortoise, he mentioned his younger sister, Mary, was looking for a job. She looks a bit flighty but she is quite all right, and worth a try." "Oh, Mrs Whittle, what is the chance, do you think, you could go and find Doug and see if his sister could come and see me as soon as possible?" I said eagerly. She laughed. "Quite right," she said, "strike while the iron's hot", and with that she took off her apron and went out through the yard to return ten minutes later with the news that Mary would be coming to see me at two o'clock.

I have to admit I was slightly startled at my first sight of Mary. Her magenta lipstick clashed horribly with her scarlet jacket, and her frizzy yellow hair and four inch high heels did not at first suggest a reliable kitchen maid. But that just proved to show how wrong first impressions can be. For having got past the rather garish trappings, I came to a pair of very nice grey eyes and a charming smile and we took to each other instantly, and indeed I engaged her on the spot. Mary was in fact a great success and a tower of strength to me over the years. She was quick and intelligent and moreover always ready to "have a go" when we were faced by one of our recurrent crises. Of course we had our moments, particularly when her love-life was proving difficult when she was liable to burst into tears and flounce out of the kitchen at the drop of a hat. But she always came back and when she finally got married to one of her more sober young men I was delighted to be asked to the wedding. When finally, six years later, we left Newport, Mary (her hair and lipstick perhaps a shade less vivid, and her heels a trifle lower) and I parted with mutual sorrow.

With an extra person around life in the kitchen became less fraught. Mary came in that very evening and coped with the bread and butter and tea side of the meal, while I sweltered over my lumps of fish. It all got done eventually and if it was not up to cordon bleu

61

standard no-one complained and it was all eaten. As I was taking off my apron, the rather spiky young resident master suddenly put his head round the door. I was frankly at that stage in no mood to hear complaints and, no doubt looking a cross between an avenging demon and the cook in *Alice in Wonderland*, I am afraid I fairly snarled my "Yes". He took a step backwards. "I thought that when the fish was cooked as usual the rumour that the cooks had finally gone must be false," he mumbled. "No," I said shortly, "but have no fear, your dinner will be served at 7 o'clock as usual." We looked at each other. "Thank you," he said finally and beat a retreat. Mary giggled. "I'll do a bit of fish and chips for you and for them before I go — I don't mind cooking for four (in fact she was a very good cook) and I don't suppose you feel much like facing it." I thanked her warmly and retreated gratefully to my house, laughing to myself as I passed the drawing-room door. It seemed what I was having to do was a world away from elegant teaparties and silver teapots.

I went up to the nursery where the children were having their hightea, and greeted me rapturously. Those early days when I had to spend long hours in the kitchen were difficult for them, used to having me around all the time. But they were wonderfully adaptable, and I was always sure I was there to read their bedtime story. On this occasion their comments were somehow typical. "Have you been having a lovely time in the kitchen?" asked my elder daughter, obviously rather enviously — being allowed into the school kitchen was always rather a treat for them. "You smell funny," accused my younger daughter. Knowing exactly what she meant I went and had a rapid bath before I embarked on the bedtime story. Finally, having seen them into bed, I went down for my own supper, very well cooked by Mary and left on the hot plate. "Very good fish and chips," announced Robert cheerfully, tucking in. But when I looked at it I suddenly could not stand the sight of it. "You have mine as well," I said — which he did, and I went up those 46 stairs to the little attic bathroom with the gas-stove in the corner and boiled myself an egg.

This particular cooking discipline did not of course last for ever, though at the time it seemed as if it did. Indeed that very first weekend I was saved from the full horror of coping with cooking every meal on my own, with the boarders in for every meal, by help from a very unexpected quarter. Going down to the gardens as usual on Friday morning to see about the vegetables for the weekend, and thankful to be out of the stuffy kitchen for half an hour, I found George in an unusually communicative mood. "Bit pushed in the kitchen are you?" he enquired. I admitted I was. "My missus cooks for numbers, you know," he volunteered. "Yes, I had heard that," I said, "but I also understood that she works full-time at the local hospital, or I would have been in touch with her." "Well, she do and she don't," he replied somewhat cryptically. "She works every other weekend, and it so happens this is her weekend off. It might be worth your while to have a word with her — she is in the house right now. Mind you I don't promise anything but she might just consider helping out — she couldn't abide the last cooks." He led the way up the garden, in through a back door of the boarding-house and up some stairs to a top flat. Opening the door he shouted, "Hi there — Mrs Glover would like a word." A sharp-faced dark-haired woman appeared smoothing down her apron. Whereupon George, having effected introductions, returned to the garden, and I got down to the serious business of finding out whether indeed Mrs Turner could help me in the current crisis. In the event, to my utter joy, she volunteered to take over the main cooking for the weekend, and also do breakfasts in the coming week as she did not have to be at the hospital until ten o'clock in the morning.

I returned to the kitchens with a much lighter step. With Mrs Turner taking over the weekend and then next week's breakfasts I was only committed to one big meal a day — the boys' tea plus, of course, lunch for the family and the kitchen staff, dinner for Robert and me and the masters, and supervising the boys' cocoa-and-biscuits supper. A few weeks ago when I thought all I would be called on to do was to sit comfortably in my own house and plan meals, this might have seemed a tough assignment, but compared with what I had thought I was going to have to do for an unforeseeable future (would I ever get a new cook?) this was relief indeed.

I returned to the kitchen to tell the good news to Mary and Mrs Whittle. Mrs Whittle was surprised. "She is a good cook," she said, "but I never thought she would do it — George don't like her taking on extra jobs in case it interferes with his meals. Mind you, they hated the last cooks, and would do anything to spite them — and I dare say, with that girl of theirs growing up they could do with the extra bit of money. Mind you," she added, as she turned back to the sink, "she will take some of the best bits back to George, but I dare say you will think it's worth it." In the event she did — and I did. For she worked hard and fast, and though I made sure the "bits" did not assume too large proportions she was worth her weight in gold to me over the next ten days.

During all this time, of course, advertisements for a cook had been appearing in the local papers, and further afield, but they were bringing in practically no response. It was a bad time, early summer, when hotels were taking on staff for the summer season ahead, and were able to offer bigger wages than I was allowed to do. Further the accommodation offered was not good — the little flat was frankly rather dingy — and the kitchen, as I was beginning to realise only too well, was old-fashioned and awkward to run. The first applicant, a smart young woman, in a navy suit took one look at the flat, and announced she certainly would not live there. The second, of whom I had had great hopes as she had told me on the phone she wanted to be near a sister at Wellington, turned the job down out of hand when she heard the hours, which were far more than she was used to, and saw the amount of kitchen help available. By Thursday of the next week I was getting desperate, as I knew Mrs Turner was having to be "on" at the hospital the next weekend, so could not help me out. Then that very afternoon, without any previous approach by phone, in shuffled Mrs Smith (I came to think "Mrs" might have been a courtesy title, as there was never any word about a Mr Smith). She was in her late fifties, but looked strong. There was also a look of strain on her face which I could not at first identify. But when I began to talk to her, I realised she was very deaf and either could not or would not wear a hearing-aid. We had a somewhat difficult dialogue, but what I believe emerged was that she was not appalled by the kitchen, or the hours; she was not put off by the flat; she was prepared to take the wages offered; AND she was free.

Crossing my fingers I rang up the referees she produced, and got the response that she was "quite a good plain cook" and she was honest. When I asked why she had left the last two jobs, I was told that in one case she had left as a result of a misunderstanding, which had arisen as a result of the fact that she was hard of hearing. In the other case, with the sensitivity of the deaf, she had taken umbrage when she thought that the youngsters for whom she was cooking were laughing at her. "She is not a bad old stick," added my informant, "if you can stand the shouting. But I have to warn you it seems she never stays anywhere very long." I thanked him for the warning, and feeling that an hour's shouting a day was infinitely preferable to six hours' cooking, I engaged her on the spot and, used as she was to picking up the routine of new kitchens pretty regularly, she made no bones about cooking the boys' tea and the masters' dinner that very day. Both meals were perfectly acceptable — and I was relieved to notice she quite expected me to lock up the store-cupboards.

After dinner that night Robert passed through the kitchens on his way back from his study and greeted the new arrival. Later he came back into the house, clearing his throat. "Have you seen her," I said enthusiastically. "She is really quite nice isn't she?" Robert grinned. "Oh yes," he said a little hoarsely, "but if I were you, I would get in a very large store of gargles and throat sweets — you are going to need them." This proved very sound advice.

My deaf lady did not stay for more than a few months, but it was long enough to allow me to draw breath and get more accustomed to the vagaries of catering for numbers, and be altogether more assured about what had to be done when. During the next three years cooks came and went, a fairly varied selection, and some more equal than others. And of course in the often unavoidable interregnums between cooks I again "stood in", reluctantly, but at least without the panic I had felt when the situation had been thrust upon me in my first week. I now more or less knew the ropes and was aware I could cope if I had to. Among the cooks I had at that time two in particular were especially memorable though for widely differing reasons. One was a man who came with splendid references (I imagine written by himself or at least a friend) who was certainly an excellent cook, but who was removed suddenly one afternoon by the police who wanted him for a variety of wrongdoings. But the cook who certainly gave most pleasure to the family, and even more particularly to the masters, was a middle-aged lady who late in life decided she wished to be a cook, and had just done a cordon bleu course. She then wanted to get experience with numbers, and as she also preferred to be in Shropshire or Cheshire for personal reasons, she was willing to take over cooking for a school, at least for a limited period. She actually stayed with us for over a year until she realised that though she was happy enough with us, she must make a move to a good restaurant or hotel if she wanted to fulfil her real ambition. On the minus side of an otherwise equable arrangement, she was, understandably enough, very extravagant — I had many a battle to persuade her that in our situation margarine really did have to replace butter. But on the plus side we had some delicious meals, and the masters were certainly never out for dinner if they could help it. As regards her cooking for the boys, this was pretty uniformly excellent and she introduced some interesting innovations. For instance on Shrove Tuesday she persuaded me to join her in the kitchen, where together we produced pancakes for all the boys as part of their tea — a very popular move. I learned a great deal from her, and indeed still have some of her excellent recipes, though, like some cooks, she was not always happy to share them. I remember guiltily how, after I had asked if I could have a couple of recipes which the family had greatly liked and had been refused, I came into the kitchen when she was off-duty and discovered that she had left her closely-guarded book of recipes on the kitchen table. I admit to a lot of quick copying and still laugh to myself every time I use those recipes, as I still do.

When my cordon bleu cook finally left, with expressions of mutual pleasure over our partnership, I was about to gird up my loins, metaphorically, for another period of unpromising cooks and a number of interregnums, when what still seems like a miracle happened. The school had a general inspection, and when they had inspected the academic side, which was now of a good standard as a result of Robert's enthusiasm and no doubt new-broom methods in sweeping out the unsatisfactory, they turned their attention to the boarding side. When they had done this they reported to the governors that yes, the boarding side was being run efficiently, but it was running at an unacceptable price. The headmaster's wife was grossly put upon, and there should certainly be no question of her shouldering the whole burden of cooking whenever there was a crisis. They then made it clear that, first the pay offered to cooks must be more realistic if they wished to attract good cooks (the governors were in fact paying considerably less than the county rates) and secondly, without further ado they must seek to appoint a deputy cook who could be local. Suddenly my world was transformed. Very shortly after that meeting I was lucky enough to find Alice, a good plain cook, who did very well and was still there when we finally left. At the same time an excellent local woman was found who could do limited hours, for whom the job of deputy cook was ideal. She too was there when I left. From my point of view, even if the job was still not quite the "nice little job you can do in your spare time and earn a bit of pin-money" as described to me at Robert's interview, it was now possible to enjoy it.

And of course it had added to my so-called skills in the kitchen, in that I have since never been frightened of numbers. But I feel I should warn any future head's wife who is offered the job of catering for the school or even a boarding house, to ask a very pertinent question, namely, "If the cook is off sick or leaves for any reason, who does the cooking?"

CHAPTER
FIVE

It never happens when I'm out

Responsibility for the feeding of 80 boys and the resident masters, which I discovered could involve cooking for all these people if there was a crisis, because there was nobody else to do it, was part of the "job" I was told I would have to do, as "housekeeper". The other part was to stand in for matron during her time off. I was to discover there could be more to this too than I had been led to believe.

Term started quietly enough. Matron arrived at my house with a large tin box containing such things as elastoplast, bandages, antiseptics, and cough medicine, and on the first Thursday afternoon, which was always her time off, I sat around in slight trepidation, waiting for something to happen. All that in fact did happen was the arrival of a rather grubby eleven-year-old with grazed knees, needing to be cleaned up and antiseptic cream applied. Nothing difficult here — I was doing much the same thing daily for my own young.

In fact the next few weeks passed without trauma — a succession of bruises to be treated with lead and opium, the odd aspirin or gargle to be given, and one quite nasty burn to be dressed — the result of a slight accident in the chemistry laboratory. There was nothing alarming here — it was in a way merely enlarging one's own family. As I had no surgery I did all my "treating" in the bathroom, and there was no doubt that this homely and intimate environment helped the boys to relax, and I got to know a number of them quite well as they chattered on about their family backgrounds and even their work problems, as I cleaned and bandaged. I have always enjoyed talking to the young, and I frankly came quite to enjoy these sessions.

Then one Thursday, after I had done my surgery which for some reason I remember was treating a wasp sting, and when Robert and I had just started supper, our front door was suddenly and unceremoniously thrown open, and a voice could be heard shouting, "Mrs Glover, Mrs Glover". Startled I got up quickly, and opening the dining-room door was confronted by a white-faced panting small boy who almost sobbed out, "Oh please, Mrs Glover, come at once, Taylor's dead."

I am reported to have said firmly to the boy, "Nonsense, of course he isn't", and to Robert, "Ring the doctor to alert him." What I do remember is running extremely fast out of the house, down the path, and into the street leading to the junior house, followed by curious glances of passers-by into whom I almost cannonned — still clutching my table napkin. Thrusting it into my pocket, I followed my guide through the house and into the garden, where in the gathering dusk on the ground under a large tree lay the white-faced and horribly still Taylor. As I reached him his eyelids flickered — at least he was not dead, but as he opened his eyes I could see from the pupils that he was certainly suffering from pretty severe concussion. I sent a prefect who had just arrived back to Robert so that he could tell the doctor the nature of the emergency, and then tried to find out whether there was anything obviously broken, before I attempted to move him somewhere more comfortable than the damp grass in the now half-light. Kneeling beside him I asked, "Can you move your right arm?" The mouth opened and the lips moved but no sound came out. "Why can't he speak?" demanded one tearful small boy standing by. By this time I had solved that one, "He is winded." I replied. "Tell me, did he fall out of this tree?" There was a chorus of assent from the little crowd round me, and one of them volunteered, "He was swinging from one branch to another and misjudged the distance. He is usually very good." I looked at the small white figure, just beginning to take painful breaths, and I looked up at the high branch of the tree, now getting quite indistinct in the gathering gloom. No wonder he had missed his grip, and no wonder he was winded. I got rid of the juniors and sent some of the seniors for blankets to put over the small, now shivering, body.

By the time the doctor arrived I had established that Taylor could move both his arms and his legs without too much discomfort, and the doctor confirmed that, astonishingly, nothing had been broken, and we got him into the house. He could now speak, though obviously very breathlessly, but he was still incoherent.

"It is a bad case of concussion," confirmed the doctor, "so he had better be watched tonight. I'll see if the cottage hospital can take him in for the night." The cottage hospital, who were always wonderfully helpful to us, agreed to have him for the night, so that their night sister could keep an eye on him, but the next problem was to get him there.

However, the doctor confirmed that he could be moved by car and by this time Robert had turned up to see how serious the situation was. So, finally, with the help of a large capable prefect called Mick, Taylor was carried to our capacious ancient Austin, where he was settled comfortably in the back with me supporting him.

Inevitably halfway to the hospital something happened which, if I had known as much about concussion as I do now, I could have foreseen and been prepared for. Taylor was violently sick — all over me. I had absolutely nothing with me to cope with the situation, except my faithful table-napkin, which I now snatched thankfully from my pocket. "What would you like me to do?" said Robert in some alarm. "Drive on as fast as possible to the hospital," I replied through gritted teeth. The journey was probably no more than five minutes in duration, but it seemed a very long five minutes.

At the hospital I thankfully handed the wilting little figure over to a sister, who, having taken charge glanced at me with sympathetic amusement — I must have looked a sight — and told me where I could wash. "I am afraid there is nothing for it but to strip off when you get home," she commented, "and my advice is that the next time you bring in a concussion you carry a bowl."

Incidentally that evening was memorable for being the only occasion on which I had ever seen Robert offer a cigarette to a boy. I had noticed vaguely, as I struggled out of the car at the hospital, that by now both Robert and Mick were looking perhaps less than their usual robust selves. But I was still surprised, when I returned to the car to find them both puffing companionably at cigarettes.

"Well, I was dying for one, after all that," said Robert, and I knew perfectly well he was a secret smoker. So I thought that just for once it would make us both feel better and I have sworn him to secrecy." At all events we all returned to school in approximately cheerful spirits.

Taylor, I am glad to say, lived to tell the tale, and indeed when his nice mother came to see me to thank me for my ministrations, she told me that what was chiefly upsetting him was the memory of having been sick all over the headmaster's wife, which was the first thing he remembered. The rest was a blank. In fact the only lasting result of that little episode was a notice written in Robert's scholarly hand, and which still remained years later pinned to the junior common-room board. It read, "No tree-climbing is allowed after lighting-up time."

That accident was no doubt the most dramatic one with which I had to cope in my role as stand-in matron, though of course there were lesser ones mostly connected with the games field, or sometimes the laboratories, but a sudden attack of asthma to which one of those early boarders was prone, or the onset of the inevitable infectious disease, which you are bound to get when you get a number of youngsters gathered together in close proximity, could bring their dramas.

The Asian flu epidemic of 1958 in particular provided a number of tricky situations, though the boarding house did not suffer nearly as badly as the day boys in this respect, partly, I honestly believe, because, to a large extent we won the war of nerves on the subject. There is nothing that puts the whole of a boarding house on its back so quickly as the belief that everyone is bound to catch whatever it is that is going round. So with the help of the boarding masters and senior prefects I started a great campaign of "There is no need to catch Asian flu if you follow these rules". The rules we instituted were two. First everyone had to gargle with salt and water every night and morning. Secondly everyone must take the halibut-liver oil capsules which we dished out every day after meals. The cost of buying these capsules on the retail market would of course have been prohibitive, but we availed ourselves of every contact we had among parents who were in any way connected with the pharmaceutical trade to discover a source which would let us have the quantities we needed at a very small proportion of the cost which I would have had to pay at a chemist. Solemnly every morning and evening prefects took "Gargle Drill" and equally solemnly after every meal the boys filed past me to get their capsules. We were of course perfectly aware that these measures would be of little avail against a hefty dose of the prevalent germs, but they certainly helped to strengthen the boys' resistance to ordinary infections, and what was more it made them feel that something was being done for them to ward off the infection, and it was therefore not inevitable that they would fall victims to the epidemic.

But despite our efforts we still had quite a large number of cases of the flu, which was a great strain on matron and, though to a lesser degree, on me. The bad cases where temperature rose very fast to 104 degrees were alarming. But some of the lighter cases, where a boy was feeling well enough to play the fool, could be equally tiring in a different way. Then there were those who like little old women were convinced that only mother's remedy was any good. This could consist of wrapping themselves in a particular scarf or sucking a raw onion and they had to be watched to make sure they also availed themselves of the remedies we had to offer. I shall never however forget one particular remedy, known as "Isaac's cure", which caused us both astonishment and amusement.

Isaac was an African boy from Nigeria, who having taken O-levels in English and Yoruba in his own country had somehow turned up in our school, with the avowed object of getting to an English university and becoming a lawyer. That this was a very long shot soon became abundantly clear as, though he was 20 years old when he arrived (indeed I made him a cake for his 21st birthday), in most subjects he knew considerably less than a boy in Form 2. But of course I only had the general overseeing of his well-being in the boarding house.

Isaac, to everyone's credit, fitted in well in the boarding house, despite his advanced years, and the boys liked him, regarding his habit of cheating at whatever game he happened to be playing as an amiable eccentricity. Then one morning, when I was helping Matron out with the unusually large surgery, Isaac appeared and, fixing me with a literally glittering eye, announced in sepulchral tones, "I have a fever." Certainly he had all the symptoms of sore throat, headache and high temperature, and I packed him off to bed. It was therefore with considerable astonishment that on that very afternoon, when I was taking my youngest for a walk in the fields behind the school, I suddenly saw Isaac, dressed in his athletic gear, pounding at a great rate round and round the next field. I called to him with horror, "Isaac, what do you think you are doing? I told you to stay in bed." Isaac galloped towards me and said in those same sepulchral tones he had used that morning, "Madam Mrs Glover, this is the way that Isaac gets rid of his fever", and he was off like a shot — and I certainly could not have caught him.

When I got back to school, I went straight to Matron and together we awaited the culprit's return. At last he turned up in a lather of sweat, and we made him take a shower and go straight to bed. But the really infuriating thing about it all was that when I came to take his temperature that evening it was down to normal, and in the morning he was back in school.

Though we hardly liked to try Isaac's "cure" on our other patients, as they might not have had such robust constitutions, I would dearly have liked to have had some of them out of sick-bay long before matron would allow them to get up, for once they were over the worst some were inclined to find sick-bay with its magazines and radio a welcome change from the classroom. By now matron was beginning to look very tired indeed, and indeed I thought she looked considerably worse than some of those lolling about in bed. But she had got to the stage of fatigue where she did not feel strong enough to argue with them and make the necessary decisions.

In the end I took matters into my own hands and rang a mutual friend, who was a marvellous cook, and whose husband had a large farm nearby, and asked her if she would consider having matron for the day — and explained why. "She needs rest desperately," I explained, "but if I merely tell her to take a day off, she stays here. I know she will keep sneaking back to sick-bay to make sure everything is all right." My very nice friend agreed willingly and said she would come and pick her up at once. So I then informed matron, brooked no protestation, and when my friend arrived bundled her firmly into the car. Having seen her safely off the premises, I then went on a tour of the sick-bays and converted sick-bays — as, with the numbers we were dealing with, we had had to adapt some dormitories into temporary sick-bays.

In the first sick-bay I found one boy looking very hot and heavy-eyed and sorry for himself, trying to sleep, one boy, still flushed but obviously over the worst, and just beginning to be able to read a little, and two youngsters having a splendid time trying to stand on their heads on their beds and making a considerable noise. In no time at all, despite voluble protestations of "But I'm ill", I had these two youngsters out of bed, into warm sweaters and track suits and along to the nicely warm day room, and I continued my progress. By the time I had finished, out of the thirty boys I had found in bed only eight remained. The others, warmly dressed, were continuing their convalescence in the day room, all looking perfectly cheerful. This halved the problem of getting food to my patients, as the food was being brought to the day room, and further I got the "walking-wounded" taking up food to those still in bed. Matron was both shocked and relieved when she returned and found out what I had done, but she had to admit that not one of the "lead-swingers" had a relapse, and quite half of them were ready to return to school the following day.

CHAPTER
SIX

A welcoming environment

When I first became a headmaster's wife I was given two very good pieces of advice from more experienced wives in a similar position in other schools. One was, "If a headmaster's wife is to do a useful job, she cannot allow herself the luxury of being shy." The other was, "Always keep the kettle on the boil." As time passed I became increasingly aware how very sound both those pieces of advice were.

I had been a painfully shy child who had to nerve herself even to open the door to go into what everyone assured me would be a "lovely party", and I have the most vivid memories of the feelings of sheer panic I endured every week when, told to go out of church before the sermon so that nanny waiting for me outside could take me home, I had to face the no doubt benevolent barrage of eyes as I scurried up the aisle, convinced I should not be able to open the heavy door. (In later years I heard Robert give some very sound advice to a prefect who found it difficult to face the battery of eyes as he went to the lectern to read a lesson: "Look firmly at them, as if you were weighing them up rather than wondering what they were thinking of you." I still recall with amusement the formidable look that prefect used to turn upon the congregation — everyone sat up. Unfortunately, I had not the benefit of Robert's wisdom when I was young.) By the time I was a head's wife, I had at least learned how to conceal my shyness, and fully understood the importance of providing a warm friendly atmosphere into which Robert could bring parents, boys, members of staff, stray visitors — where they could talk in a more relaxed environment than his study, with the further relaxing accompaniment of appropriate things to eat or drink.

The completely unexpected ones were obviously the most difficult but metaphorically "keeping the kettle on the boil" and the sherry decanter and gin bottle always replenished — with of course the availability of cakes and biscuits and "bits" to go with drinks — one got used to taking them in one's stride, though one had sometimes to get over the embarrassment of knowing one was looking less than elegant when some such visitor appeared. If one is, for instance, looking after a school kitchen or enjoying one's children or one's garden, one cannot always look as immaculate as one might wish. I have, for instance, been caught by elegantly-dressed parents coming into my garden where I was happily at work attired in a filthy pair of jeans, saying, "Sorry to disturb you, but we just wanted a word and could not make anyone hear when we rang the bell."

Even worse, one evening, when I had just washed my hair, Robert, without any warning brought in some parents whose car had broken down, saying he had told them I would be only too pleased to give them a drink or some coffee while they waited for their car to be mended. All I could do was to wrap my long dripping hair in a towel, cover it with a scarf and go and dispense coffee and cakes and small talk. But as I sat there with little trickles of water running down my neck, and well aware I looked a perfect sight, I comforted myself with two thoughts. One was that as a result of this exercise I might well get a cold, and so get a day in bed, which at this stage of the term was wholly desirable. The other was that they were so understandably concerned with the inside of their car that the chances were they did not really notice.

Finally there was one more thing I learned if one was to be able to cope with unexpected guests at any time, and that was one should never have chops for lunch. This was first brought home to me one morning in the holidays in our early days at Newport, when only shortly before lunch I had a message from Robert's study to say he was bringing the architect to lunch — and it was chops. There is no way I know of making chops stretch, and as it was the school holidays there was no-one from whom I could "borrow" one, and it was too late to send out for more. In the end I called my two small daughters, explaining the situation to them, and saying that though it was simple to make scrambled eggs for one person, if those eggs were being eaten at the table, it might well embarrass our guest

83

who would realise he was eating someone else's chop. So we tossed for it, and Jane, our second daughter, won the toss and declared herself very happy to have scrambled eggs, of which she was very fond, in the nursery — and we would explain she was not at lunch as she wasn't feeling too well.

All went to plan, and the architect, himself a family man, was sympathetic. A little later in the afternoon however I suddenly saw him passing through the garden, where Jane, looking the picture of health, was swinging herself very high on the swing. The architect looking mildly surprised, asked, "Are you better?" and I waited with bated breath for Jane's reply. I need not have worried. After only a momentary pause my quick-thinking daughter replied with a dazzling smile, "Yes, thank you — it never lasts long." Both little girls then rushed into the house to collapse in giggles at this magnificent charade, which had made their day.

I never risked chops again and I think rightly for our architect admitted, when we got to know him better and years later shared the joke with him, that at that stage of our acquaintance he would indeed have been embarrassed to see a member of the family eating scrambled egg while he demolished what would have obviously been their chop. So much for unexpected guests.

Of the entertaining I was expecting to undertake, one main category was of course the boys, starting with the new boys. For over twenty-three years, nearly every Sunday afternoon during term-time, four o'clock to six was reserved for new boys' tea parties when four little boys, scrubbed and shy, had to be put at their ease and then listened to on the subject of their hobbies, their holidays, their families, their pets, and of course all the accidents that had over their short lives befallen them. From the tales I have been told you would never believe how prone small boys are to accidents, and from my point of view, how fortunate, for accident stories are the most wonderful ice-breakers. You have only to start one young visitor on the tale of "how he got that scar", and the others, shyness forgotten, would be clamouring to cap it with a tale of what had happened to them, their families and their friends, and the ice would be broken. Once the floodgates were opened you hardly had to say another word, except of course "Have another piece of cake", as their lives unfolded before you. I think many parents would be surprised at the things I know about them, including one very nice mother whom I never saw subsequently without remembering her son's matter-of-fact voice saying, "My mum is lovely but she's a pathetic cook."

Of course the right food for these parties had to be provided. I was determined that what they ate was home-produced food rather than school food, which was very difficult in the early days at Newport. However after three years — after the inspection in fact — the Haberdashers built me a little private kitchen, and then it became much easier to provide all the family favourites. I must have made a veritable ton of chocolate cake over those 23 years, from a good-tempered recipe which never seemed to mind being left in *mediis rebus* while I coped with this or that crisis in family or school kitchen, but rose cheerfully and evenly once I had time to get it into the oven. Other favourites in our family tended to be known by the names of the donors of their recipes (I am a great recipe collector) so that I would have the pleasure of hearing one of my young guests saying quite seriously, "May I have another piece of Mrs Hume, she is delicious" or, "I love Mrs Biggart" or, even better, "I am afraid I find Mrs Gilkes a bit hard for my loose tooth". And of course no party was complete without its allotment of chocolate biscuits whose wrappers could, if carefully taken off, be re-wrapped round air, and replaced on the plate in the hope of fooling the next would-be biscuit eater — another sure-fire ice-breaker.

These tea parties were quite a lot of work, but there is no doubt that interesting non-school food contributed to the feeling of relaxation and well-being, and I was amply rewarded by the conversation that began to flow as the plates got lighter — there was rarely anything left however much I put out. What is more, our home had obviously become a pleasantly familiar place to them, and, even more important, my husband could be seen as a friendly human being after all. Certainly I enjoyed being hailed in a fellow-well-met sort of manner as I walked about the school after I had had these small boys in.

Boys between the third form and the sixth form I rarely entertained — it was kinder on both of us. From being frank chatty young mortals, boys, particularly in the fourth and fifth forms, tend to go through an unsociable stage. Instead of coming up to me as I passed through school with a cheery remark, the boys who had chatted so easily at my tea-table a few months before, suddenly preferred to pass me with averted eyes and the minimum of formal recognition. But my experiences with boys passing through this stage enabled me to reassure anxious parents who were worried about the behaviour of their early-teenage sons. "John used to be such a sweet boy," they would say, "but now he is so rude and difficult, and does not seem to want to do anything we suggest." At this point I could assure them I had seen many "Johns" pass through this stage, and provided parents remained firm but calm they would ultimately emerge perhaps different but just as nice.

By the sixth form the boys were again prepared to be sociable and now we invited them to lunch preceded by a glass of sherry in twos and threes. Each year we would start with the head of school, who during his time in office nearly always became a real friend of the family, and work our way through monitors, school prefects and house prefects. As at this point of their career boys were constantly leaving, as they obtained their university places, so that others were "made-up"; there was no end to it, but it was, on the whole immensely enjoyable. Sometimes the conversation was a little above my head, particularly if they discussed scientific matters, but over the years I became enormously impressed by the way the boys would hold politely but firmly to their opinions, as discussions ranged over a great variety of subjects. Robert loved discussion and argument, and was genuinely delighted with someone who held firmly to an opinion in opposition to his own, provided he did it calmly and with good manners. Years later I was particularly pleased when meeting an old boy, now in his thirties, at an occasion unconnected with the school, he turned to me and said, "You know it was at your lunch table that I first discovered the pleasures of adult conversation." That certainly made me feel that even those more difficult sessions when one had to work hard to keep the party going were definitely worthwhile. These young gentlemen, learning the pleasures and art of conversation were still in many ways, however, the same individuals who five years before had emptied the plates of cake and scoffed all the chocolate biscuits, in that they had not lost their appetites. I never failed to be amazed at the quantities of food they managed to stow away. I learned to lie bravely: "No, of course I have nothing in mind for that joint — do finish it between you." And it went without saying that there was never a crumb left from the two different puddings I had supplied for their pleasure. But the charming letters many of them wrote to thank me for having them made the decimated joint seem supremely unimportant.

Apart from Sunday entertaining, Saturday late-afternoons were a time when our drawing-room tended to be a magnet for a succession of boys. Robert, who was a devotee of all sports, particularly those connected with a ball, always wanted to be told, first-hand if possible, every detail of every match. As a result the room became filled with a succession of boys all bearing score-books or copious notes. Armed with these they either gave a detailed explanation of everything we had seen happen in the match that afternoon (all headmasters' wives must be prepared to spend every Saturday afternoon on the touch-line, the boundary or the river bank according to season) or, if it had been an away match in which our informer had been taking part, there would be a blow-by-blow account of every tackle, every try or every run and ball bowled and catch taken, or, alternatively, it seemed, every stroke rowed. Robert was a marvellous audience answering enthusiasm with enthusiasm, while I gently pushed teacups, from a constantly filled teapot, and, of course, the odd biscuit in their direction. But just occasionally, unfortunately for them, he had to be away. On these occasions the residuary legatee did her best. It was a disappointment to the boys, but even I was better than nothing provided I listened with wrapt attention, nodded sagely and expressed the appropriate emotion and, very important, wrote everything down in a notebook I kept for the purpose to show Robert. Actually I quite enjoyed these sessions, and became quite knowledgeable about "coming round the blind side" or "off-breaks", and for a dizzy spell I actually knew the difference between junior senior crews and senior junior crews.

The last occasion in their school careers when we entertained boys was when they were leaving, and I held a succession of leavers' parties. I remember the first time Robert broached the subject that it was a thing we should do, we had been at Newport for just four terms and my reaction had been, "I can't possibly do it — it's the end of term when I shall have all the preparations for feeding people on speech day." "Well you can't do it before, as they will be in the middle of exams, and you can't do it afterwards or they will have left," replied Robert with irrefutable logic. I could see I was fighting a lost cause, if he had made up his mind, so I asked in some trepidation, "How many would there be?" "Oh, about fifty, and you need not give them anything very sophisticated," was Robert's airy reply. "It just can't be done," I exclaimed in horror. However two large hams, several chickens, a mountain of salad, an assortment of sweets and several jugs of a mild wine-cup later, I realised it could be done and was probably worth the effort. Not that these parties were uniformly successful, though the majority of those who had got through to the sixth form had genuinely enjoyed most of their school careers, were indeed mildly sentimental about leaving, and wanted to talk about their futures — and these were delightful. But in addition to these there is, I am sure in most schools, a "lunatic fringe" who can't wait to leave school, and are anxious to demonstrate their distaste for the whole system before they leave. Just occasionally some of these, asked along with the others, though with a sinking heart, would turn up with the intention of "sending-up" the party. These could be very wearing, giggling in corners, laughing raucously at private jokes, and helping themselves to more wine-cup without being asked. Mostly, as they were so much in the minority one could ignore them, but I do remember once being driven out of my "hostess" manner to say wearily, "It will be awfully nice when you grow up." Actually this remark, to my surprise, caused such deflation that I felt rather — but not very — guilty afterwards. But at least it appeared to remind them very soon that they had buses to catch (they were all day boys) and the party resumed its comfortable tenor. Actually persuading the party to go at the appropriate time could be a problem. Partly it was because they were obviously enjoying themselves — I have a warm memory of a very nice country boy looking at his watch and saying, "Oh good, I needn't go for another fifteen minutes to catch my bus, if I run." But it was partly that they did not know how to get up and go without appearing rude. One would put firmly on the invitation "7p.m. to 9.30p.m." but it made no difference — the shadows lengthened and still they talked, very delightfully, but we were getting tired and there were things to do, like getting tomorrow's party on track. In the end we used to have a private arrangement with the senior boy present — the head boy or a head of house — to give a lead. I remember some splendid histrionic renderings of "Good gracious, how time flies, it's high time I was back in the house". This usually worked, though I do remember one occasion, when we were both very tired, Robert suddenly getting up and saying, in desperation, "Well, I am sorry to break up the party but I really must get back to my study — I haven't finished my speech-day speech yet". But even that did not work. They all rose, thanked him politely, and as soon as he had left the room, they all smiled at me and sat down again.

Entertaining the young was therefore very much part of our lives, and it is obviously easier for a headmaster if there is a residuary legatee to share the load and indeed stand in if he is called away, as can happen. But Robert always felt, and I am sure he was right, that it was important for masters and their wives, to feel that the head's house was a welcoming comfortable place. So we always opened our house on Sunday mornings to anyone who felt in need of a cup of coffee after chapel. Numbers varied considerably (though there were always the hardy perennials), according to the stage of the term, the weather, and the popularity of the preacher, so that I was glad I had inherited from my Scottish grandmother a certain "feyness" which seemed to be able to predict reasonably accurately what sort of "house" we should have. Though I have to say sometimes even Granny nodded and I found myself, while my guests waited, rushing around boiling kettles and mixing "real" with "instant" in a carefree manner. However these were always pleasant informal occasions, so a bit of delay really did not matter, and we got to know very well those who came regularly. Though even so, I suppose young masters coming for the first time could have regarded it as a bit of an ordeal, and at first certainly one or two were obviously a bit nervous until they got to know us better. I remember particularly one delightful young man who had the misfortune on his first visit to knock over and break his saucer — of course I assured him at once that nothing could matter less — I always had more saucers than cups. However he then followed this by somehow dropping and breaking his cup — again I assured him that it was of no importance it was certainly the one with the crack in it. Finally he capped it all by knocking over and breaking a favourite Venetian glass ashtray. This time I was spared thinking of a reason why this too was so singularly unimportant by his trying to pick up the pieces, thereby cutting himself and bleeding all over the place. At this point I led him rapidly to the kitchen rather as if he was one of our 13 year-old tea-party boys, and cleaned him up. As I stuck on some plaster he said miserably, "I seem to have a sort of hoodoo on me." "Then we must break it," I said firmly. "Come to supper on Saturday." So he came and carried in my best coffee set, and nothing disastrous happened — so we reckoned the hoodoo was well and truly broken.

In summer, and particularly when our children were young, these coffee parties sometimes had an extra dimension. It happened that one Sunday morning was such a particularly lovely day that we took our coffee into the garden, where our children, at that time aged between five and ten were enjoying a variety of cricket. Richard, the five-year-old had newly acquired a cricket bat and he was standing in front of the stumps while his sisters bowled a little inexpertly at him. After a series of very wide wides, one of the young masters, with the most tactful charm, asked if he could "have a bowl". As the ball now began to arrive within the batsman's reach this was a tremendous success and suddenly we were all, or mostly all, involved. Sides were picked and battle joined to the obvious pleasure of all parties. Moreover the pattern was repeated, at Richard's earnest request nearly every fine weekend until the end of term — and again the next summer. It certainly gave the children immense pleasure — and also afforded them profound astonishment that the scores made by the opposing sides nearly always turned out to be identical, which caused great merriment. Though towards the end my elder daughter obviously began to think there was something odd about it. She took me aside on one occasion and said seriously, "You know, mummy, I believe Mr Paris was trying to get out." "Perhaps he wanted his dinner," I said dismissively. "We had better not say anything to the others."

In addition to open coffee mornings we also, when time allowed, tried to fit in small supper parties, particularly for new masters and their wives, so we could get to know each other. Naturally, some went better than others, often depending on how socially at ease the wives were. To help me have some basis for conversation with the wives, I tried to study carefully any relevant curriculum vitae that was available, but there was one occasion when I remember very clearly that I slipped up badly. Three young couples had arrived together at the beginning of one autumn term so I decided to have them all together, and the party was going quite pleasantly. However I noticed that though two of the wives were chattering happily mostly about the exploits of their children — as sure-fire an ice-breaker as "accidents" are with small boys — one of the wives was rather reserved. So, trying to bring her into the conversation I asked brightly, "I have forgotten, is yours a boy or a girl?" There was a brief silence and then the young woman said, very solemnly, "We have only been married six weeks." Well, we got past it, and when in a year's time I went along to admire the first baby we were able to laugh about it.

Finally in "family" entertaining came the governors. The only occasions when I had to entertain all of them together were of course speech days, when somehow I fitted between twenty and thirty people into our dining room (I liked if possible to mix in a few local people with them) with the help of various tables borrowed from all over the school. But I was also expected to give lunch to the deputation of Haberdashers who came every term to attend governors' meetings. I have to admit I was terrified the first time I had to do this, but as we got to know them, and there were some very distinguished as well as very nice men among them, I came to enjoy these occasions and I know Robert felt it eased his path to be able to relax with his governors, particularly if a meeting had been a difficult one. I have always thought good food and drink are great calmers of tempers, so I used to try very hard on these occasions (I remember hearing my elder daughter telling someone very solemnly, "Mother believes in food"). But it has to be said that for some years the smoothness of the party depended not only on the quality of the food, but the success that various members of the deputation had had in getting through a pet scheme, or, even more, on the state of the back muscles of a particular member of the deputation. He had been a wicket keeper of some distinction, having

played for the Gentlemen against the Players some
years ago, and on damp days his back gave him
considerable pain. On these occasions he would quarrel
with anyone who was near him, so I began the practice
of always sitting him on one side of me. He was
unlikely to have a go at me, and if he did I wasn't likely
to take offence. In fact I developed quite an affection
for the old man, whose rare praise was worth winning.
It was for him especially I sought out the best Stilton. I
remember very well him looking disparagingly at it
once and saying in a voice of deep suspicion "That isn't
Danish Blue, is it?" To be followed by a snort of
laughter as I replied cheerfully, "I would not dare." It
was for him I finally got round to making cushions for
those beautiful but uncomfortable chairs in the
dining-room. But even he was unaware of the history of
a certain pudding which won his particular praise. I was
called out in the middle of the second course by a
scared-looking Mary who led me to the kitchen where
in the middle of the floor, on the remnants of a broken
dish, sat a particularly handsome looking Queen's
Pudding, obviously dropped by cook as she took it out
of the oven. Beside it was cook having hysterics, and the
kitchenmaid trying not to laugh. Obviously something
had to be done rapidly, so turning to the three of them
I said, "Mary, get out our prettiest dish and two fish
slices and lift that pudding into the dish as carefully as
you can. Cook, get out and open a tin of mandarin
oranges and a tin of apricots and drain them. Mrs
Whittle beat up that carton of cream. The thing to do is
to fill the interstices with the fruit and the cream." To

cook's credit, she stopped having hysterics with something practical to do and I left her busily repairing the damage and returned to the dining room. "Any problem?" asked Robert looking a little worried. "No, no," I replied airily. "Cook had cut herself and they could not find the plasters. It is all sorted." Eventually Mary brought in the pudding and I have to say it looked delectable and tasted delicious — cook had done a wonderful job on it — and was widely acclaimed. I could not resist looking at Mary who was serving and saying, "Please convey our compliments to cook — it is a lovely pudding." Mary's lips twitched but she replied gravely, "I am sure cook will be very pleased to hear that." Years later I won a prize in a woman's magazine for my suggestion of an "extra" quality a good hostess should have in addition to the obvious ones. "Unflappability" I had suggested. "If the guests do not know that anything has gone awry and they are not eating exactly what had been originally planned, they will enjoy whatever you put in front of them, as long as you appear relaxed." I had learned the hard way.

Local governors we entertained less formally and in both schools developed a very happy relationship with some of them. But in particular I remember with pleasure the old Bishop of Shrewsbury who had been so kind to me and put me at my ease at the time of Robert's interview. Governors' meetings often took place at 5.30 in the evening, and quite regularly on these occasions between 5p.m. and 5.15 I would hear the front door open and a voice call, "Anyone at home to give an old man a cup of tea?" He was very fond of children, and knew that nursery tea was generally going on about then, so he would stump upstairs, have a joke with the children and review the teatable. He was usually lucky as the children were devoted to him and always reminded me to have his "favourites" on governors' meetings' days. I have a happy memory of him setting off downstairs with an egg sandwich in one hand and a brandy-snap in the other, pursued by my elder daughter with a paper-napkin. "You must take this to wipe your fingers on," she said earnestly, "or you might get your notes sticky." He enjoyed this very much and promised to do as he was told.

CHAPTER
SEVEN

All comers

Every school, particularly a boarding school, has a fairly constant stream of visitors, coming to preach, to lecture, to give concerts, to examine music pupils. to inspect the C.C.F. — the list is endless. And there is no doubt that anyone coming to give a service in this way will have more of a chance to do it to the best of their ability if they can relax beforehand in a comfortable place and, if appropriate, be also metaphorically fed and watered. A school waiting room is not the ideal place for this, so once again who is more ideally placed to minister to their comforts than someone with a house on the premises happy to cope with whatever and whoever turns up — in fact that residuary legatee, the head's wife?

As long as one has notice (and that notice can be very short on occasion) day visitors are no problem. But of course some need overnight accommodation — such as weekend preachers. These are usually very nice people and again no problem. In this category I remember with pleasure and affection an old Oxford friend of ours, one of the best preachers I know, and a great favourite with the boys, sitting me down firmly

99

while he finished off the flowers for my dinner-table (which he said with perfect truth he arranged better than I did) and then making a delicious sauce to go with the main course. I also remember an absolutely delightful, very Welsh, preacher who, when Robert complained that when in Wales he was sometimes disconcerted by Welsh people relapsing into their own language which he did not understand and wondering what they were actually saying about him, produced a Welsh phrase which said in effect, "I understand everything you are saying". Robert on several occasions with an insouciant air and a charming smile used this phrase to great effect both in small Welsh shops, but even more on the rugby field when the coach was addressing his team.

But not all preachers were so agreeable, and I remember one in particular who caused me considerable problems. As we sat down to dinner on Saturday evening, he looked coldly at the prawn cocktail in front of him and announced firmly, "I am a strict vegetarian." I thought glumly of the lamb to follow and the ham for tomorrow's lunch, and my heart sank. By the time he left I felt he must almost look like a piece of cheese.

Ex-headmasters and their wives who came regularly when the ex-head could talk to boys about possible careers, were naturally enough usually very understanding guests — they had been there. Certainly I have warm memories of Hugh Lyon, ex-headmaster of Rugby, when coming downstairs and finding me laying up the table for dinner, immediately saying, "Come on, chuck me the silver and get back to your kitchen — I'm a splendid pantry-boy." Though I have to say that among other visitors I recall a couple who arrived just as we had come back from holiday to find that the painters, having mistaken the date had already moved into our only double guest-room. We did the only thing we could and offered them our room, while we withdrew to the caravan, but the situation was made more complicated by the fact that a mosquito bite I had acquired the day before suddenly blew up necessitating a visit to hospital. Our visitors were very understanding about the fact that dinner was rather late, but in the same breath informed me that the wife really preferred to have her breakfast in bed in the morning. I was so flabbergasted I remember I actually gave it to her.

Lunch-time guests came in all shapes and sizes, ranging from music examiners to politicians, who again might range from Victor Feather to Lord Raglan. It was very stimulating and one learned a lot, though from the hostess's point of view these visits could also provide anxiety, as the time schedule was always very tight and nothing must run late.

Gerald Nabarro caused a mild crisis by wanting tomato juice. I had plenty of tins of "shop" juice in the larder, but Robert actually caused the problem by saying airily, "Oh, you MUST try some that Jean makes herself — it is really good." Certainly I had some, but it was in the deep freeze, and while my guest waited expectantly and the minutes seemed to go past at an alarming rate I struggled to unfreeze the wretched stuff to a drinkable state. At least it needed no ice in it.

101

Further regular lunch-time visitors whose tight schedules always caused some anxiety were the representatives of the army and air force who came annually to review the C.C.F. The children particularly enjoyed these visitors because they were so colourful with their gold braid and their red tabs, but I always had to be sure to get lunch through in sufficient time to enable them to get "dressed up" again, in their belts and swords, all competing for the mirrors like a lot of debutantes.

Teatime entertaining was mostly limited to headmasters and their families coming to warm themselves up after a rugby match against one of our teams. Mostly, as we got to know these heads and their wives better, these were very pleasant occasions, as we all caught up on the gossip, even though one always had to start from the point that we had just played a match and one of us had won, and the other lost, and one or two took it rather hard.

After a few years at Monmouth, something happened which increased the amount of entertaining I was expected to provide — but in a most exciting way. A music society, known as the Merlin Music Society was formed, whose members would pay subscriptions to hear concerts of the very highest standard. The Haberdashers had recently built for the school a very fine new hall, which could provide the ideal venue for these concerts, and Robert offered this to the society with the proviso that boys who wished to come to concerts could do so at a very reduced rate. The school's musical director, one of the founders of the society, looked after the actual organisation of the concerts with great efficiency and the catering department undertook to look after half-time coffee, but of course somewhere was needed where the artistes could rest beforehand, be fed before or afterwards, according to taste, and sometimes be put up for the night. The residuary legatee was delighted to oblige.

It was fairly hard work, as I also held a small party after the concert, where those who had performed could wind down, as well as giving members of the committee a chance to meet the distinguished musicians. But I admit to finding the whole experience most rewarding and well worth those hours of preparation. Interestingly we discovered, not for the first time, that those at the peak of their profession were nearly always our easiest guests. Those who had not quite reached the heights were often more difficult. I remember with enormous pleasure Elizabeth Schwarzkopf sweeping into our drawing-room with that kind of warmth and charm one associates with the Queen Mother, and exclaiming how she had enjoyed the audience, how pretty the room was, how thoughtful the arrangements made for her comfort, and how nice of us to put on this party. We all basked in the glow of her warm personality. It had indeed been a magical evening, with her singing Lieder as only she can sing it. At one point she had appeared to be singing particularly to one small boy in the front row, and I asked her about this. She threw back her head and laughed. "Poor little soul," she said. "He had the hiccoughs. I thought that if I sang to him he would forget his hiccoughs and as he relaxed they would go away." "Did it work?" I asked. "Of course," she replied. Certainly her singing was "breathtaking" that night.

On the other hand, another quite well-known, but not so very well-known, soprano was memorable in another way. I asked her what she would like to drink, and she had replied, somewhat surprisingly, "Whisky on the rocks", which rather offended my Scottish soul. Being without any help at that time of the evening (the remembrance of that original headmaster's wife of many minions often went through my mind on these occasions) I hurried off to the kitchen to get some ice, no doubt fumbling with it in my desire to be quick. When I returned to the drawing-room only a few minutes later I found my guest, certainly surrounded by admirers but looking straight in front of her, tapping her foot, and muttering, "Where is that woman with my whisky?" Feeling like an incompetent barman, as I suppose I was, I thrust the glass into her hand and turned to cope with the other twenty-odd guests who were awaiting my attention. I believe she thawed slightly after the whisky but I have to say I was not interested enough to find out.

On the whole we found that the artistes preferred to eat very little before a concert, particularly singers, but enjoyed — some of them obviously really needed — quite considerable quantities of food afterwards as well as company to help them "wind down". Dennis Matthews was an extreme case of this. He wanted nothing but half a glass of water before a long and demanding Beethoven concert, but after the concert, was ready and eager to settle down, even at 11 o'clock at night, to a sizeable meal and a bottle of wine and talk at length most interestingly on all manner of subjects until the small hours. On the other hand I did entertain one soprano who viewed with obvious disfavour the light meal I had provided for her before the concert, and announced she always sang better on a steak. We always asked the agents for information about performers' eating preferences, but even when they gave us information, I have to say it was often completely inaccurate. So, despite the lady who wanted a steak, I generally made the practice of providing a reasonably light meal beforehand, making it crystal clear that it was entirely up to them whether they ate it or not, or indeed asked for something I had not provided, or whether they ate something after the concert, or indeed did not eat at all. This provided for most contingencies, and I have a delicious memory of John Lill making himself instantly and delightfully at home on these terms. He was one of those who preferred to eat before a concert, but had arrived at Monmouth with only time to manage one course. After the concert he obviously enjoyed the party and helped himself to all the refreshments I had provided, and when the other guests had gone, said he would like to stay a little longer to relax before his long drive back to London as he was not able to stay the night. "Is there anything else I can get you?" I said at this point. "You didn't have time to have much dinner." He smiled engagingly. "That chocolate mousse I didn't have time to eat, it looked awfully good." I brought in the bowl, and he finished the lot with evident enjoyment, talking away like an old friend of the family, before he heaved himself up and got on his way. Some years later he came again to play at the school, this time at very short notice, filling in for someone who had been taken ill. I opened the door to him before the concert and immediately he exclaimed with pleasure, "Of course, now I remember, Monmouth means chocolate mousse — I knew it meant something nice."

It has never been my lot to launch a thousand ships, but to be remembered with appreciation for the products of one's kitchen is better than nothing. On one occasion we had that very special accompanist, Gerald Moore, to give a lecture recital, which was followed by one of my usual parties. Some five years later I found myself sitting next to Gerald Moore at the Dorchester on the occasion of a luncheon given by a lecture agency for speakers and luncheon club officials — of which I was one. I had no reason to expect him to remember me, who was after all just another hostess among the hundreds who had entertained him over the years. However I said, a little diffidently, "I heard you give a lecture-recital in our little town of Monmouth some years ago, which I enjoyed enormously." He put down his soup spoon and looked hard at me. "I knew I had seen you somewhere before." A beatific smile spread over his face. "Of course," he exclaimed "Brandy-snaps — they were delicious."

Indeed, recollections of our delightful if brief association with some of the world's greatest players and singers are too numerous to mention, and from some we actually received great kindness. Of these the most memorable was Benjamin Britten, who meeting my daughter Jane, then in her teens, and, as he told me, realising that she was someone special, gave her enormous pleasure by sending two tickets for his *Peter Grimes* with Peter Pears in the title role for her next birthday, whose date he had elicited from me.

Of course, as we were not responsible for the programme, not every concert gave such pleasure. For instance neither of us, and particularly Robert, were great fans of very modern music, and as we were entertaining the artistes afterwards we could hardly walk out of a concert, however much we disliked what was being played — not obviously anyhow. I have to admit however there was one occasion when we had an extremely loud jazz concert and Robert decided he could not stand any more and did not return after the interval. When the artistes came into our house later for the usual refreshments, they inevitably asked him how he had enjoyed the concert, to which he replied with grave courtesy that he had enjoyed the second half of the evening more than the first. Fortunately this seemed to satisfy everyone.

More often, however, it was not so much the concert as the party afterwards which could produce problems, which were often associated with language difficulties. I, regrettably, am no linguist and could do little more than struggle in schoolgirl French and minimal German. Robert was better and considerably bolder and with the help of a number of friends who were proficient linguists we were usually able to cope fairly adequately with artistes who came from Western Europe. They were generally very charming and very courteous, and I learned to submit almost to the manner born to having my hand kissed — at least after the first occasion when I was taken by surprise and, trying to shake the hand of a particularly charming Italian violinist at the same time as he was trying to kiss my hand, gave him quite a hefty punch on the nose. But when it came to musicians from Russia or Eastern European states we could run into real problems. If they had an interpreter, as they quite often had, or if at least one or two of them spoke a little French or German or Italian, we managed to battle on with the help of smiles and gestures. But there was one party of Bulgarians who completely defeated us. None of them had any French or German and the only two English phrases they had between the eight of them were "Good evening" and "Whisky please", which limited conversation. The so-called interpreter was worse than useless. She could speak a little Czech, which one of her protegés could also speak, but she had no Bulgarian at all. Her sole contribution was to announce on arrival that her party had been very put out when arriving at their hotel they had found how expensive whisky was — so she had promised there would be whisky at the party after the concert. Rather unfortunately it so happened that, very unusually for us, we had two bottles of rather good whisky (brought back recently by friends who had been abroad from the duty free) sitting on the sideboard for all to see. I hoped that perhaps a couple of rounds might satisfy them — but no way. Having

108

eaten all I had to offer, which was considerable, they kept appearing at my side holding out their empty glasses, and finally one of them actually picked up the second, newly-opened, bottle and retired with it and three companions to the other end of the drawing-room. I was speechless with fury, but felt that as a good hostess there was little I could do. However our splendid head of school, who used to come in to "buttle" on these occasions, had no such reservations. Murmuring grimly, "This has got to stop", he advanced on the group round the whisky bottle, and with a charming smile and a pantomime of gestures indicated he needed the bottle at the other end of the room. He then picked up the bottle, and with considerable sleight of hand made it disappear into the folds of his voluminous monitor's gown as he turned back. He then made a brisk retreat to the kitchen, emerging a minute later without the whisky. He then began very obviously to stack up the empty plates, cups and glasses not in use, indicating as firmly as he could that the party was over. Eventually our guests took the hint, final "Good evenings" were said, and they were shepherded out.

A "problem evening" of rather a different nature arose only a month later. On this occasion the artistes themselves were in no way to blame. A very good orchestra was giving a concert and, as usual when it was an orchestra, I had only asked in the conductor, the soloists and the heads of the sections as these were really all I could comfortably accommodate. As far as the others were concerned refreshments from the school kitchen were sent round in the interval, and afterwards many of them went to the pub on the corner and were quite content. On this occasion there had been some sort of a slip-up in the catering department, and no refreshments had reached them in the interval which justifiably annoyed them. This had come to Robert's ears as he was coming back to the hall after the interval, so he went round to see them and make our apologies. He finally rejoined me in the hall just as the orchestra were filing back into their places and told me what had happened, adding, in the most casual manner imaginable, "I did not want them to get a bad impression of the school, so I've asked them all into our house afterwards for a drink and a bite." He then composed himself peacefully to listen to the second part of the concert. I was speechless with horror. With glazed eyes I began to count the numbers of the orchestra as they slipped back into their places . . . thirty seven, thirty-eight, now the conductor, thirty-nine, plus the soloist, forty. I already had asked a number of friends of the school to the house to meet our guests, and with them it would make a grand total of fifty — and I had catered for fifteen. I did not hear another note of that concert as my mind struggled with the problem of how to make my few loaves and fishes go round. Certainly the cakes I had made for Sunday's new boys' tea could go into the pool, and the Quiche Lorraine I had made for tomorrow's supper, and the mince tart I had made for tomorrow's lunch and the meringues designed for Sunday lunch. As for something to drink, the women usually went for tea or coffee and I could cope with that if I moved fast enough, but undoubtedly the men, who had been playing all evening would want beer and I had not nearly enough of that. And how about glasses and cups and saucers? Gradually the jumble began to subside in my mind, and I began to make a plan of action, as I gazed surreptitiously around to see who was present who could help, and spotted the assistant caterer (thank goodness she was musical) and two useful housemasters. The moment the orchestra had taken its last bow, I was out of my seat like a flash, and grabbed the assistant caterer and the housemasters who agreed to find me the necessary glasses and cups, hissing at Robert as I went, "Get hold of a crate of beer — somehow." (He says it is the only time he has actually sent boys into a pub.) Then I fled back to the house with the imperturbable head of school and two senior monitors in close attendance. We worked like demons boiling kettles, cutting up and assembling on plates everything I could think of that would fit the bill, and by the time the first member of the orchestra arrived I was in a state to welcome them with reasonable calmness, saying how lovely it was to see them, and how much I enjoyed the concert. (I am told I was heard to agree with someone that the second part of the concert was particularly enjoyable.) At all events everyone appeared to enjoy the party, which was the point, and were complimentary about the wide range of "eats" provided. Usually after one of these parties, when all the visitors had gone, Robert and I used to settle down with the helping monitors to talk over the evening over a fresh brew of coffee and the rest of the food. On this occasion however there was precisely one small sausage roll which had somehow got overlooked. So there was nothing for it on this occasion but to make a large bowl of scrambled egg, which I have to say went down very well after all our dramas.

To be happy, willing and able to entertain all comers is certainly a fundamental duty of a head's wife and all comers come in all shapes and sizes, from our delightful and very efficient maintenance engineer who obviously enjoyed dropping in for a cup of coffee and a chat about antique furniture, about which he was quite knowledgeable, to the very occasional member of the royal family.

Our first royal visitor was Princess Margaret who had close connections with the Haberdashers' Company. Arrangements had been made that she should be entertained to lunch by the local militia in their headquarters which were on the site of the castle where Henry V was born, then tour the school in the afternoon and finally come to tea in my house where I was told she would also like to meet some of the boys as well as local worthies.

I was very lucky at Monmouth to have as my helper in the house for all but the first few months of our time there, a splendid person who in fact became a friend of the whole family. Sturdy, reliable, humorous and unflappable with a tremendous zest for life she proved to be the perfect person to help me with the often unpredictable situations and amount of entertaining that came my way. I shall never forget how on one occasion I was entertaining some unexpected guests for dinner, but because I had called on her good offices so often lately, I felt I could not call yet again on her free time and good will on this occasion. I was therefore astonished to come into the kitchen to change the courses to find Mrs Wellington standing at the sink washing up the saucepans. Looking up slightly sheepishly she said, "I knew you felt you could not ask me yet again, but you know I just could not settle to my knitting thinking about you, so I said to my old man, 'She'll never manage that lot on her own' and I got him to run me down."

On the occasion of the royal visit, Mrs Wellington was in her element. While I worked away at the cakes and scones she polished everything within sight until it shone. I still remember her stumping down the stairs announcing with satisfaction, "Well she won't have a better polished lavatory seat even in Buckingham Palace."

Mercifully the visit went very well. Princess Margaret did not sample much in the way of the cakes I had made but the rest of the party, a mixture of local worthies and sixth-form boys, did full justice to them, and I had been careful to find out what brand of tea — and cigarettes — she favoured. My two daughters did the "waiting", ably supported by Mrs Wellington who I heard having what can only be called a matey and entirely unselfconscious discussion with the Lord Lieutenant on the rival merits of drop scones and shortbread. Meanwhile the princess had established a tremendous rapport with the sixth formers with whom we had surrounded her. I heard one of them telling her with pride about Monmouth's prowess on the rugby field. The princess eyed him with mild amusement. "And what happens to those poor little boys who come here and don't like rugby?" she enquired. "By the time they have been here for a term or two they will like it," came the firm reply, and I admit I looked a little anxiously at Her Royal Highness to see how she was taking this. However she laughed very pleasantly, and her lady-in-waiting who happened to be standing by my side at the time said with obvious satisfaction, "This visit is going very well, Her Royal Highness is obviously enjoying herself."

Another royal visitor, some years later, was Prince Charles who, coming to Monmouth to address a meeting in the school hall on the subject of conservation, was to use our house as a rest place to gather his thoughts between having luncheon with the mayor in town and making his speech. The prince breezed into our house at great speed but somehow with the air of a young man who has had a hard morning, so I showed him straight into the dining-room where he could be quiet with his aide and a cup of coffee for as long as he needed. Meanwhile the rest of his small entourage which included the Lord Lieutenant, the High Sheriff and Lady Anglesey, who was his technical adviser, settled down in the drawing room to chat companionably over their coffee. After fifteen minutes or so Lady Anglesey said, "His Royal Highness obviously does not want any more information, so I might as well get out of the way and take my seat in the hall", and she left to walk the short distance.

114

However she had not been gone for more than a few moments when the aide erupted into the room saying the Prince wanted to talk to her urgently to confirm some point about which he was going to speak.

I immediately got hold of one of the gaggle of policemen adorning our front door, explained what had happened and asked if one of them could find Lady Anglesey, tell her the problem, and escort her back — and thought the problem was solved. But it wasn't. Minutes ticked by and no Lady Anglesey appeared, and the aide, now looking decidedly anxious, came in again to see what was delaying her. Again I retired to the front door step to ask what the problem was — to be met by the sheepish reply, "Our man in the hall doesn't know what she looks like." So I called my elder daughter, Kate, who did know what Lady Anglesey looked like, and proposed to send her up to the hall, only to be stopped by the sergeant who explained she would not get in without a pass as security was very tight. In the end, to the amusement of a small crowd who had gathered, a slightly self-conscious Kate set off at the double for the hall escorted by two large policemen, one on each side of her, to return triumphantly a few minutes later at walking pace this time with Lady Anglesey, and still escorted by the two large policemen. Finally, the speech finished, His Royal Highness re-emerged, calm and restored and prepared to joke about the multiplicity of doors in our drawing-room, as he emerged through one door and his aide through another to meet unexpectedly face-to-face. "Bit like a French farce this," remarked the Prince.

Royalty, world-famous musicians, distinguished politicians, these of course were the high spots of our entertaining, but it seemed to me during those years the drawing-room was never empty for long, as one concourse of people followed another. (But, as Mrs Wellington used to say, "It's one way of keeping the moths out of the carpet.") After all a large room in the middle of a small town cries out to to be used for charity functions, especially if it belongs to a school that wishes to be part of the life of that town. And so it became usual for the NSPCC, the Church of England's Children's Society, the local cancer committee and the local Cheshire Home committee, to name but a few, to hold their various "events" in our house — so much so that Mrs Wellington, polishing up the furniture once again, would say, "You must tell me again who it is today — I do get 'em mixed." Indeed to try and give each charity a separate "image" I would try to get the charities to stick to their own particular brand of hospitality, sherry parties for one, coffee mornings for another for instance, and I remember particularly the NSPCC liked to stick to teaparties for which their committee members produced the most delicious cakes, so they were very popular, and to give these teaparties an extra "edge" I would try and dream up a different "theme" every year. For instance I remember a Rainbow Tea, a Topographical Tea and even a Common Market Tea, all of which produced some splendid cakes from recipes researched by their committee members. Inspiration for these themes tended to come to me in the bath, though it has to be

116

said that by the time I left Monmouth, after years of dreaming up ideas both at Newport and Monmouth the baths were tending to become longer and hotter.

Actually almost the jolliest party we ran was at Newport for the Church of England Children's Society one halloween. The old house there really lent itself to such a party with its big halls and old staircase, and I got tremendous help from the young man, who was one of the boarding masters, who ran the art department. It was near the end of term and he was delighted to get his junior classes making all manner of black cats and creepy spiders, and on the night of the party he came with a senior class rigging up a witch (alias one of Kate's dolls) floating on a broomstick over the staircase and an invisible curtain of black threads which brushed the faces of arriving guests. All in all it was a most successful party. The Children's Society did very well out of it and the locals were still talking about it when we left Newport two years later.

So the kettle was rarely off the boil, and as for my notorious childhood shyness, it got lost — it had to.

CHAPTER EIGHT

Public events

Apart from being always on hand to be ready, willing and able (and look happy about it) to entertain in her home all comers, the residuary legatee must of course be prepared to do all she can to ensure the success and well-being of public events connected with the school, the chief of these being the annual speech day. Of course the formal part of speech days — the church service, and the ceremony of the prize-giving and reporting on the school's progress was nothing to do with me. However when you have a lot of people gathered together for the greater part of a day, it is important for them to be fed coffee, lunch and tea at the appropriate times if they are going to be relaxed and enjoy themselves. The responsibilities I had to undertake varied considerably between the two schools of which Robert was headmaster. In Monmouth I was expected to look after the speaker, and often his wife, overnight which was in nearly every case very enjoyable as we had some very charming as well as distinguished speakers, and to see to the needs of the governors and their wives for coffee and lunch on the actual day. But at Newport, being in effect the school caterer, my duties went much further.

I shall never forget our first speech day at Newport. During the summer term Robert brought our splendid second master through to the house so that he could explain to me what would happen and what part I would be expected to play.

Obviously the formal part of the day — the arrangements for the church service and the prize-giving — was all under control; as Mr Taylor said, he had been doing them for so many years he could do them in his sleep. Though even here I was filled with apprehension as he told me that, as the school had not at that time any building large enough to house all those who wished to attend the prize-giving ceremony, this took place on the lawns in front of the school. "What happens if it rains?" I asked with some horror. Mr Taylor took his pipe from his mouth and replied mildly, "It doesn't; I can't think why but it just doesn't." Suffice it to say that indeed for the next five years, when we had no alternative accommodation for the parents but the open air, it threatened — but never actually rained. Though oddly enough when, in our sixth year, we had built a gymnasium large enough to accommodate the ceremony, it poured all day. But all those years thinking about the possibility of rain added a certain piquancy to one's arrangements.

As in many schools, the speech day celebrations started with a service in the church, attended not only by boys, masters, parents and local governors, but also by a large deputation from the Haberdashers'

Company including the current master, his clerk, the beadle and members of the court, who processed colourfully in their robes from school to the church across the road watched by a large number of onlookers. After the service and a short formal governors' meeting, while parents presumably found lunch somewhere in the town (and here anyway the majority of the boys were day boys), the deputation and local governors were given a formal lunch in school. "I presume in my dining-room?" I asked. There was a short pause while Mr Taylor pulled out his pipe. "Well it is a little difficult," he finally said. "For the last two years the rector's wife has asked if she can help out by having some of the governors to lunch in her house — the school sends over the food." "Local governors?" I asked. Her husband was after all a local governor so this seemed very reasonable. "Well, no," replied Mr Taylor, in obvious embarrassment. "She prefers to have the master and wardens." I set my jaw. "I am sure she means to be kind," I said, "but over my dead body." He looked alarmed so I added, "I promise to tread as delicately as Agag."

The opportunity presented itself a few days later when I happened to meet the rector's wife in the fish shop. I advanced on her with what I hoped was an ingenuous smile. "I do hope you will forgive me dispensing with formality and, as I have met you, ask you here and now if you and the rector will give us the very great pleasure of lunching with us on speech day," I said. She looked decidedly nonplussed and replied, "Perhaps you have not heard but I usually share the

120

honour of entertaining the principal guests on speech day with the headmaster's wife". "Oh, but I could not dream of your doing that," I said, all eagerly innocent. "You work so hard for the parish, and it will be so lovely to have everyone in our house for Robert's very first speech day." What could the poor woman do? After I had brushed all her objections gaily aside, she grudgingly consented, and I went home in triumph to tell Robert who was very amused. To give her credit, she bore no malice, and after that first lunch, perhaps not a culinary triumph but reasonable enough, as we powdered our noses together in front of my mirror, she said very graciously, "You did that very well, my dear", which I appreciated enormously, and from then we developed a very pleasant relationship.

The lunch — for 22 people — of course produced its own problem — to find something a bit special, easy to cook and serve. It was the time of a very plain cook whose only idea was "a nice roast chicken with bread sauce". But chicken gets dry once it has been carved — and in any case who was going to carve it? However chicken of some sort — not heavy and unlikely to be tough — was a good idea, and for the weeks before speech day we experimented with various ways of cooking chicken for the masters' supper — Chicken Maryland, Poulet Sauté Hongroise, Coronation Chicken — but always there seemed to be part of the process cook got wrong. In the end I devised a dish which I knew she could do faultlessly, and as it was an amalgam of a number of recipes I called it "Poulet Alicienne" (her name was Alice) which pleased her enormously

121

and very much amused my now good friends among the Haberdashers' governors. As time went on I became more adventurous in my menus, myself always taking on the provision of special puddings as I knew by now my Haberdashers' governors had a great weakness for puddings — and indeed eventually earned myself the title of "The Lady of the Puds".

At Newport however my responsibility for catering did not stop with lunch — it had apparently always been the tradition that tea for all boys and parents should be provided by the school, which according to Mr Taylor had always been "pretty shambolic". Vowing at least to improve on the shambolic I spent the last weeks of term trying to cope with a seemingly endless list of things to be ordered, from extra china, urns, and biscuits, to squash for little brothers and sisters, and at the same time find time in the kitchens by simplifying menus, to cook fruit-cake and cookies that would keep. I cannot pretend that in the end the serving of teas went without a hitch, but I was heartened by Mr Taylor coming up to me at the end and saying, "That was much better."

Then there were the flowers. I have to admit I am not one of those clever flower people. Any self-respecting flower which I am trying to arrange inevitably falls flat on its face. However there obviously had to be flowers in my house and on the platform. The flowers themselves were no problem as George Turner wheeled up a great mass of roses, stocks, delphiniums, red hot pokers, ferns and leaves. Much more of a problem were possible containers and I raided the

122

kitchen for any pan or saucepan they were not using, and even went round classrooms collecting the kind of waste-paper "basket" which holds water. Incidentally over this I was approached after the ceremony by one of the very senior masters who, fixing me with a gimlet-like eye, said reprovingly, "I have just seen my waste-paper basket on the platform filled with delphiniums." Next year when I went to look for it I found he had found some way of padlocking it to his desk. The sweet-peas with which I had decided to fill my house, as George grew particularly fine ones, posed another sort of problem. It had been agreed between us that as it was hot and sweet-peas tend to wilt, George would not bring them up in the morning before speech day but I would myself come down in the evening and fetch them. However I was so busy in the evening I sent down a very nice fifteen-year-old to ask George for them and remind him I wanted long stems.

Very unfortunately the boy chose to use his initiative, for, not finding George in the garden and having a knife in his pocket, he decided to cut the flowers himself but, not being a gardener, instead of cutting individual flowers he thought it would be quicker to cut the whole stem two or three feet down, and arrived back at my house carrying what appeared to be sheaves. I looked with horror. "Does George know?" I gulped out. "Yes, I seem to have done it wrong," the boy replied. "What did he say?" I went on. The boy looked mystified. "Well actually, he did not say anything. It was rather awful. He just threw his cap on the ground and pointed me to go away." As soon as I could I went to see George who was now trying to sort out the destruction. I said my piece to which he said not a word until I turned to go, and then he said through gritted teeth, "Just don't send that varmint near me ever again or I won't answer for my actions."

When I got back to the house our speaker for tomorrow, the distinguished president of Robert's old college, had arrived and was having a lively conversation with my two daughters, which they were obviously all enjoying. "I've been asking him if it's difficult to make a speech," announced Jane, "and he says the only thing you must not do is to say 'er'. So I shall listen hard." Mercifully it had always been the custom for the speaker and the headmaster to dine with the Haberdashers at their hotel the night before a speech day, so I was then left in peace to lay up my table with the motley collection of silver I had managed to collect from family, friends and even the school secretary as laying up for 22 guests was way beyond my own resources.

I was delighted to see that speech day dawned bright and fair, and I had just got through my morning duties and changed, preparatory to going across to the church, when cook erupted from the kitchen clutching a bowl of cream and in a state bordering on hysterics. Apparently she had beaten the cream with such enthusiasm that it had turned to butter. It was no problem to get more cream from a shop near the school but she utterly refused to try again, somehow convinced the same thing would happen. So standing in my hall, in my pale-blue suit, hat and high-heeled

124

shoes, with Mary holding an apron round me, I beat that wretched cream to the right consistency, then once more, furtively licking a tiny bit of cream from my little finger, proceeded down the path towards the church. At the gate a small crowd had gathered to see the colourful procession of Haberdashers in their full robes, and as I passed through was highly diverted to hear one woman say to her friend, "She doesn't look bad, but I don't suppose she has had much to do all morning but make up her face." I am quite sure she did not understand the beam of pleasure I directed on her.

While my guests drank coffee in my house after the service I had decided to introduce a little ploy, which indeed I used every year for the 22 succeeding years while Robert was a headmaster. Wanting to give the day a feeling of festivity, and also bring my family into the excitement of which they longed to be a part, I had ordered a quantity of rosebuds of varying colours, which my daughters went round offering to my guests. This was was a tremendous success, and when my family were grown up I continued the practice with first-formers.

Lunch followed without disaster, and the speeches were listened to in warm sunshine, and by this time I was able to sit back and enjoy them. By now of course I knew what Robert was to say, as I had heard it many times, and still was very proud of it, and our distinguished guest gave a splendid speech full of wit and wisdom. Mingling with parents at tea time had its problems as I struggled to put names to faces, but almost without exception parents kindly introduced

125

themselves to me with their name — the exception being a formidable lady who, coming up to me and fixing me with a basilisk glare, said abruptly "Now you know who I am, Mrs Glover — we met at a concert three weeks ago." Needless to say in my terror the name would not come whereupon she repeated it slowly twice — making me feel one inch high. There is always one. Robert managed better, for when some completely unknown parent approached him asking anxiously, "Headmaster, do you think John will pass his Latin?" I was delighted to hear Robert reply blandly, "I have great hopes of him", which appeared to give complete satisfaction.

At last the guests had gone and the Haberdashers had been driven away to catch the London train, and Robert and I and the speaker returned a little wearily to the house to be met by Jane in a state of high excitement. Rushing up to our distinguished guest she clasped him by the hand and announced, "You said 'er' seven times — I counted." For a moment I held my breath and then our guest with a hoot of merriment collapsed into a chair, laughing heartily. "I'm so pleased someone listened so intently," he said, "Was the rest all right?" "Oh yes," answered my four-year-old sententiously. "Apart from that I thought it was VERY good."

Speech days at Monmouth meant much less work for me, and I enjoyed preparing the formal lunch myself. Salmon straight out of the Wye from our local poacher was always demanded and solved the problem of the main course. Incidentally I had been recommended to approach that poacher for the freshest salmon by the police themselves, who later wisely appointed him as the "gamekeeper" for that stretch of the river, and he was very successful. But even in Monmouth of course odd problems arose — such as the year that both the girls who were to look after my guests at table went down with a virulent tummy-bug. However my daughters, now in their teens, performed the task with such efficiency and charm that it was a particularly good party.

Just occasionally, but very rarely, the speakers could throw up problems, though mostly to do with times of meeting them off trains. In fact the only real slight problem came not from the speaker one year but from his wife, who, just as we were gathering to go up to the church in the morning announced, "I am afraid you will have to wait for me. I have just laddered my tights and must go into Monmouth and buy another pair." There was a startled silence, but mercifully having two teenage daughters to whom similar things happened, I had a spare unopened pair of tights in the house and the situation was saved.

The nearest, in fact, we got to a possible crisis from a speaker was one of our last speech days when Sir Thomas Armstrong — under whose baton in fact we had met at the Bach Choir at Oxford — was the very lively speaker. In the church service in the morning, I had been amused to notice him quietly "conducting" the psalm being sung by the choir when on his knees. When I referred to this to his wife afterwards she said, "Oh, I was so relieved to see him doing it. If he had thought your director of music was not doing it as it should be done, he was quite capable of striding up the church, seizing his baton and taking over himself." Well done our director of music.

CHAPTER
NINE

Greasepaint in the sherry

Any headmaster's wife will obviously be only too happy to offer any talent she has, great or small, for the benefit of anything going on in the school. Some heads' wives, for instance (though I am afraid not me), have a real gift for flower arranging, which can greatly enhance the appearance of a school hall where a function is going on. In my case the small talent I could offer, and offered with great pleasure, was a certain amount of expertise with stage productions. Whereas Robert always maintained with great regularity, "There is no greasepaint in my blood", and certainly, though he obligingly escorted me to the theatre from time to time, he tended to drop off in the less well-lighted scenes, I on the other hand had become hooked on any kind of drama from the age of five when I made my debut on the stage as a sprite — no lines but lots of expression.

Through school and university and later in Yorkshire and Canterbury I acted my way between babies in tragedy or comedy — anything that came my way — and for a dizzy spell was actually asked to act with the repertory company resident in Canterbury. And it was in fact in Canterbury that I discovered my talents could be useful in school productions. For when the school was putting on a production of *The Merchant of Venice*, the headmaster, the redoubtable Fred Shirley, who had seen me act at the Marlowe Theatre, roped me in to assist his large rugger-playing Portia (who was incidentally a very good actor) to move like a woman. So at any time in the weeks before the production came off I could be seen walking round the cathedral precincts with "Portia-Adams" as he became known.

When we moved to Newport I discovered my opportunities to act with the local dramatic society restricted by such unwritten laws as the one which declared it was wholly unsuitable for a headmaster's wife to be kissed in the stage by an assistant master, so the casting had to be changed. Luckily I was asked to join a county drama group who provided actors for the Ludlow Festival, where I was just another actress, and was at one point lucky enough to be asked to play Everyman's mother at the Festival. My "son", a charming and well-known actor called Sebastian Shaw, was at least thirty years older than I was — but what is make-up for? Meanwhile I did my bit at the school helping with costumes and props, and of course making sure the cast was fed.

At Monmouth however I soon discovered that there were all manner of gaps which they were looking for someone to fill as "there is no-one else to do it". The first of these was thoroughly startling — they wanted someone to play Iolanthe in the Gilbert and Sullivan opera which the producer was longing to put on, and could cast with ease — except for the title role. Monmouth had a tradition of putting on Gilbert and Sullivan operas at regular intervals, with considerable success, mainly, I thought, because the second master, the producer, was a devotee of Gilbert and Sullivan and took the leading roles himself with tremendous distinction, having a splendid voice and also being a very fine actor. Other masters happily played other solo parts, and the wife of a semi-retired master had for years played the middle-aged roles there are always in the operas with much success, while the young heroines had always been played enchantingly by young boys. Mr Hatton, the senior master was due to retire the following year, but before he went he desperately wanted to put on *Iolanthe* — which I had to agree was one of the best of the operas. A really splendid boy had been found to play Phoebe, the middle-aged master's wife was longing to play Buttercup, and Mr Hatton was so much wanting to play a final Lord Chancellor before he retired. The problem of course was to find an Iolanthe — more of an acting part than a singer's and with a range really outside that of a treble. Then I appeared, as far as Mr Hatton was concerned, the answer to prayer. I was approached: "Please, there is nobody else and it really is an acting part rather than a singer's."

I was absolutely torn. The role of Iolanthe is not a large one and it is a delightful role to act. On the other hand I was only too aware I was not a singer — having only what my mother once described as "a good choir

131

voice, dear" (she could sing!). However I let myself be persuaded — it was after all just another residuary-legatee-there-is-no-one-else-to-do-it job, and with the help of our very nice head of music I managed to produce the notes with some sort of volume, though I still doubt whether I was heard much further back than the tenth row. I was also allowed to cheat a little. On the occasion when Iolanthe has to give a cry of anguish on a top F sharp, I was allowed merely to do a dramatic cry of anguish — which we all found less nerve-wracking, particularly the conductor. After all, we argued, Henry Lytton used to do that sort of thing, so at least I was in good company.

In actual fact I enjoyed the whole experience very much, and even at this distance I have two very clear memories which in their very separate ways still give me pleasure. One concerns the "fairies", most of them trebles out of the school choir who also that year seemed to be members of a junior rugby team — and forwards at that — so though they looked quite delightful and sang beautifully they were pretty solid, and as they began their first chorus, "Tripping hither, tripping thither", the boards of the stage began to creak ominously. Then the "fairy" leading them all on actually did trip with an unfairy-like crash, and the silver circlet which bound his curls fell into the audience. I have to say that to their credit the whole chorus behaved with impeccable professionalism, and continued as if nothing untoward had happened.

The other memory is very different but in my opinion was a little peak in my acting career. At one point Iolanthe in despair hurls herself upon the breast of the Lord Chancellor singing (or, I admit in my case declaiming) "I am thy wife." This is not an entirely easy thing to do when you are acting in front of an audience which includes a large proportion of the school and you are the headmaster's wife and the chancellor is the second master. However Hugh Hatton, who was certainly one of the best actors I have ever had the pleasure of acting with, maintained, quite rightly, that, "We've got to play this for all its worth. If we use any half measures credibility in our characters will be shaken and we shall be lost." So we played it for all it was worth, and I record with pride there was never so much as a titter. Indeed the boys who came to tea with me the following Sunday informed me very seriously, "It was terrible when we thought you were going to die. It was so sad my little sister cried." I ask for no more.

However this appearance of mine as Iolanthe was, to use modern parlance a "one-off". I continued to be happily involved in school productions but my activities were confined to less exciting participation, producing props and bits of costume, helping with make-up, and of course audience promotion.

As the first performance of a school production approached I have always been aware of the shifting eyes of the English master in charge of the production looking in a predatory way round my drawing-room, while he sipped his after-chapel cup of coffee on a Sunday morning. Sooner or later he would drift up to me. "That chair over there. You wouldn't consider lending it to us for the second act would you? It would look awfully good." We always did lend whatever they wanted of course, unless it was something very fragile or very precious, and during plays our drawing-room tended to look quite denuded. There was one particular sofa that seemed to spend as much time on the stage as it did in our drawing-room. So much so that on one occasion I remember Richard coming home for half-term when he was at prep school and looking round the drawing-room and saying in a resigned sort of way, "Well, either we are in the hands of the bailiffs or there is a school play on."

Clothes too had a way of finding their way into certain productions, particularly long skirts and hats, and I was always rather relieved that I had small feet, as even the youngest boy playing a girl could not get into my shoes. I was also initially asked if I would help with the sewing of costumes and, if I had been the slightest good at sewing, of course I would have done, but — being blessed with ten thumbs — and those double-jointed — I really could not offer help with any degree of confidence and was thankful when it was left in the far safer hands of the matrons. But there was one specialist field in which I was really needed — that was make-up.

Most plays put on by schools tend to have large casts, and few common-rooms have more than two or three men capable of doing make-up, so this small skill of mine, learnt mainly during my brief association with a repertory company was always in demand, and I enjoyed using it. In particular of course I was always asked to make up "the girls", and I can claim to have

134

produced some really devastating "ladies", particularly at last performances when skins weather beaten on the rugby field had become softened by the creams I had been massaging into them. People often asked me if the boys minded being made into girls — but to that I could always give a positive "No". For these boys were after all actors, and fully realised that to act a girl was just another character part, as much as acting an old man or an invalid, and I found them both interested and critical — in a nice sense — of my efforts. "I think we had a bit more high-lighting on the top of the cheeks last night and it was better", I remember one of them saying objectively, staring at his face as if it was someone else's. There were times of course when I had to do more than a little masking, especially when it was a Saturday evening performance and there had been a rugby match in the afternoon, for one really cannot have one's heroine appearing with even a minor approximation of a black eye.

From make-up I was naturally asked to progress to wigs, though I protested this was really not my forte and only did it when there really was no-one else. Fortunately after a few years at Monmouth I was delighted to discover that the wife of one of the new masters had actually been a hairdresser, and only too pleased to use her skills on the boys' wigs. So we worked as a team and felt we really achieved some quite creditable results. We also undertook to see the dresses were ironed — and here the matrons were invaluable and took pride in ironing the costumes between performances. So between us we got the cast looking

135

quite professional which was good for everyone's morale.

From there it was but a small step for me to be asked if I could ensure that my "ladies" looked as good in motion as they did standing still. In other words they did not give themselves away by walking with a feet-out, typical boy's walk across the stage, nor by sitting down with hands on knees. So any time before the opening night of a new play I might be seen in company with three or four boys all concentrating fiercely on walking along an imaginary straight line, and sitting down and standing up elegantly whenever we came to a bench. The better the actor, of course, the more determined he was to get it right, and they needed no persuasion to be shown how to do it.

When dress rehearsals started, the producer used to ask me to sit at the back to see if there were any awkward spots which a fresh eye can often see, and this gave me the chance to see my make-up and costumes under the lights. Needless to say I loved my involvement with the whole thing. Performance nights were particularly exciting. I had been there myself so could sympathise with the sweating faces I was endeavouring to make up, and could play up to the desperate little jokes they were making to try to prove how calm they were. With a small cast we did all the make-up together in the green room, but with a large cast space could often be a problem. So in later years at Monmouth we got into the habit for the boys I was to make up to come down to my house, only yards away, where I held my make-up "salon" in my brightly-lit kitchen. This for me had the added advantage that even as I worked away on their faces, I could keep an eye on my stove. For my stove was connected with another side of my involvement with school productions — my efforts to promote audience recruitment.

I have always thought it was important that actors should have as large an audience as possible, and as mixed as possible. It is definitely easier to sink one's own identity in a part if the audience is a general one, not one made up solely of one's fellow-pupils with perhaps the odd parent. Therefore it was important to have a leavening of completely non-committed people just there to enjoy a play.

At Newport this leavening was on the whole supplied by the town itself. It was traditional to come to school plays. But at Monmouth I soon noticed that plays seemed to be attended almost solely by school and parents with perhaps the odd governor. I could not fail to notice indeed that in Monmouth there was a mild town-versus-gown tension, no doubt stemming partly from a certain feeling in the town that when the old Monmouth Grammar School became independent it gave itself airs and was no longer part of the town. I felt that in fact this was a complete misconception, but this town-and-gown thing was something which the residuary legatee might be able to do something to address. While the producer and his associates started a vigorous campaign in the local press to stimulate interest in school plays, with quite good results, I did my bit to ensure a larger audience by "bribing" governors and a list of people known as "friends of the school" — who got invited to speech days — and anyone else I could think of who might be interested, to come to our house beforehand for sherry and "bits" to bolster their spirits at the beginning, and a sort of buffet theatre supper in our house afterwards as a reward. This experiment was such a success and so many people showed interest that in order to accommodate all the people who wished to come to the play party we found ourselves having to go to the play every night with a different lot of people. This was a considerable ordeal for Robert, not being a playgoer himself, but he bore it bravely, especially if I made plenty of sausage rolls and cheesecake for the buffet afterwards. He said the thought of them got him through the last act. On the whole the plays were well produced and well acted and I genuinely enjoyed them even at the third time of asking, except on one occasion when for some reason our English master elected to produce *The Alchemist* by Ben Jonson.

When I first saw the run-through at the dress rehearsal I though I must have been feeling very tired as I really could not make much sense of it. But even on the first night I still could not make a lot more sense, and glancing along the rows of blank faces of the rest of our party, I realised they were having the same problem. At the interval coffee break, where usually people make appreciative comments, it was obvious that everyone was having a problem in finding something nice to say. The set was a safe topic — it was a very good set so they could all enthuse about that. Then they would venture "a very interesting play" and rapidly change the subject. Suddenly a charming Australian friend of ours broke the deadlock. "Well, I suppose all you clever people know what this is all about," she announced cheerfully, "but I didn't understand a word of it, so I wish someone would explain." One by one people began to giggle. No-one had really understood what was going on, and were very relieved to be able to admit it.

But Robert and I had two more nights to sit through. So, first thing in the morning, Robert got hold of the producer and asked if he could produce some sort of résumé of what was supposed to be happening in the play, a kind of child's guide to Ben Jonson. The producer came back with an excellent neat short résumé of what was happening in the play, and Robert had it duplicated and handed out with the programmes. But to make assurance doubly sure in our own party, knowing that sometimes ladies who really needed glasses to read small print did not bother to put them into their evening bags, Robert used to give our party a verbal "briefing" in the accepted army manner before we went up to the hall. The last two nights went very much better, but, at Robert's request I don't think our nice producer ever tried to produce Ben Jonson again, at least while we were there.

We always encouraged our own "play party" to wear evening dress for these evenings to give the whole thing a sense of occasion. The half hour of drinks and chat before what Robert unrepentantly called "kick-off" put them into a party-mood and gave them time to find out from the plans we displayed exactly where they were sitting. We would then be notified by the head boy that all was ready and escorted to the hall with me leading and Robert doing his sheep-dog bit at the rear. At last we settled them in their rows, where they made a good solid front to the audience, which is important for actors to have, and over the years they became very good at leading the applause for the set, and the laughter for the first funny lines — a great asset. We always noticed that comedies went particularly well when the colonel of the local regiment was there. He had a splendid resonant laugh.

The arrival of guests at seven o'clock, or, with the keen ones some minutes before, did sometimes produce problems for me, in that it put me on a very tight schedule. Having got the room ready and the food prepared, I always expected my first clients for make-up at six o'clock, immediately after boys' tea. Normally this gave me just time to get everyone made up and out of the way before the first guests arrived, but if a problem arose with a recalcitrant wig, or I could not get someone's shading right, my guests could be on me before my clients had departed. On these occasions I could get rid of the members of the cast out of my back door, so that they did not meet their "audience" too soon and so spoil their effect, but I still needed a few minutes to tidy myself, even though I was already dressed under my overall.

One evening I remember I cut it too fine. As I stretched out my hand with a plate of cheese straws to offer them to the mayoress, I saw her eyes widen with surprised alarm and looking down at my hand (which I always used as a "palette" when I was making up) I discovered it was still covered with a lurid mass of blue lake and grey. I hastily apologised and explained, but the mayoress continued to look pained. "I don't think I want anything to eat," she said.

CHAPTER TEN

Out and about

I soon realised that if there was to be real harmony between a school and its local environment, more had to be done than just welcoming people in: one must also go out and about meeting as many people as possible, and joining in local activities.

In Newport getting to know people in the town was made relatively easy by the good offices of the rather formidable but, as I came to find, kind-hearted wife of the local rector. A week or two after we had moved in she gave a tea party to which a seemingly very large number of local ladies were asked, and I found myself firmly introduced to each in turn. It was something of an ordeal, particularly as I had not realised that at that time "hats were worn" by ladies attending Newport tea parties, so I had the unnerving experience of entering a room of people staring at me "improperly dressed". However they were very kind and I nibbled away at my cucumber sandwich and balanced my fine china teacup, and did my best to answer their questions while desperately trying to sort out who was who.

During the rest of that first term, similar tea parties took place in the houses of the ladies whom I met on that first occasion, where I had almost identical conversations — it was rather like playing over an old film again, but once I had got myself suitably "hatted" it was really very pleasant and by the time the summer was over at least I knew who was who, and also what sort of activities took place around the town, and at least an inkling of what was expected of me. But one particular tea party stands out in my mind as a really splendid period piece. At the very first tea party I was approached by a lady who bore an almost uncanny resemblance to Margaret Rutheford in one of her more eccentric roles. We got off to a less than auspicious start when she asked me in a conspiratorial whisper whether I was an expert in flower-painting by any chance. When I had to admit I was totally unable to paint anything she looked profoundly shocked, and said severely that in her day all "gals" were taught to paint — it was one of the accomplishments every young lady should have. However on my rather desperate rejoinder that I was of course very interested in other people's paintings, she cheered up at once and promptly asked me to tea for the following week, at the same time expressing the hope that the "dear headmaster" would be able to accompany me. I knew of course exactly what the "dear headmaster" would say if I let him in for that sort of hen-party, but I tactfully replied I was sure he would love to come if he could, but I was sure she would realise that there was so much to be done at school at the moment that I was afraid it was out of the question, and I hoped she would understand. Anyway next week, on my own, I went along to tea at what turned out to be a perfect gem of an Edwardian house complete with antimacassars, little footstools and serried ranks of rather indifferent water-colours on the walls. Having eaten my cucumber sandwich and tiny cake, I was then sat down with a large album of flower paintings. I think they were probably well done, though I am no judge, and I did my best to be appreciative, though after a while I began to run out of adjectives to express my appreciation. At last I got to the end and with a final "quite delightful" prepared to rise — but the ordeal was not over yet. "Just a moment, my dear," whispered my hostess conspiratorily — she was resplendent on that occasion in a sort of mauve and white smock topped, although it was her own house, with a kind of Edwardian boater — "here is something which I think will really surprise you", and she produced for my delectation another album in which the flower pictures were made entirely out of pieces of appropriately coloured stamps. It was very cleverly done and my hostess must have had unlimited patience as well as very skilful fingers, but I was very relieved Robert was not present. As a keen amateur philatelist he would, I know, have been appalled at the use to which some very fine stamps had been put. "I sell them on calendars and Christmas cards for the Church Bazaar," continued Miss Dixon, sibilant in her enthusiasm. "I do hope you will buy some." "Of course," I exclaimed, "please put me down for a dozen", and I escaped into the mundane world from a fascinating glimpse into the past.

A final, rather frightening, memory of those early tea parties was on the occasion when I first had to have these very well-meaning ladies back, as I was singularly ill-equipped for it. Being married in the war I had not had the chance to be given either dinner or tea services and the only cups and saucers which might be acceptable were an odd half dozen I had picked up in a sale. That limited the size at least of my parties. But the teapot was even more of a difficulty. My alternatives of chipped china or aluminium obviously would not be acceptable, and in desperation I rang up my mother. "You had better borrow my 'number two'," she suggested. "It is very pretty, it belonged to your grandmother, but it does leak a bit. However pour quickly, and stand it on a plate and you should get by." So when the teapot arrived I issued five invitations and began preparations. The teapot, now polished, certainly looked the part, and I did my best with little cakes while the "dear headmaster", being a better hand than I am with a bread-knife, cut sandwiches of superlative thinness. I had not, alas, got any dainty linen tea napkins, but Smiths supplied a pretty line in paper ones and I hoped I would get by.

The guests arrived, the "dear headmaster" sportingly put in the briefest of appearances (he could not have stayed anyway — there was not a cup for him) and the party got under way. On the whole it did not go too badly except for two things. The paper napkins were obviously NOT a success. "Oh yes, paper napkins," fluted one of my guests picking one up with obvious distaste. "So much more convenient for a busy mother." Loss of marks there, I thought. And it has to be said that the pretty teapot was a real headache. I had not brought it in until I was ready to pour tea, but having poured the first cups I made the great mistake of filling it up. Presently I became aware that one of my guests was looking at it with an expression of surprise and no wonder. It was now sitting in quite a pool of water. "Oh dear, how careless of me," I said, laughing idiotically, "I seem to have spilt tea all over the place", and with that I snatched up the tray and vanished into the bathroom which was next door. I then pressed everyone to a second cup, which mercifully they accepted, and this time remembered not to refill it. At last they went, all of course being very nice to me, but as I dried the tray for the last time and threw away the despised napkins, I decided there was nothing for it but to do a round of auction sales. I was lucky. At a small house sale in the depths of the country I acquired, among other things, quite a nice-looking silver-plated teapot and a collection of very pretty little tea napkins. "What silly things," commented my down-to-earth second daughter. "One bit of jam and they are done." However, silly or not, I now felt better equipped to cope with the next round.

So much for trial by tea party which, once I had realised just what was expected of me, allowed me to get to know some very nice local ladies, who asked me to join various charity committees — very important for public relations. But there was also trial by dinner-party to go through if one was to be seen to be doing one's job of integrating into the local community. That too produced problems of which I originally was not aware. Having been asked out by two very nice local couples to an evening meal, I decided it would be the right thing to have them back pretty smartly, as I had a cook at the time. So I sent both couples little notes asking them to dinner on a particular night, and was pleased when they both accepted. But what I had failed to register when they had sent their invitations to me was that at the top of their invitations were little notes saying "dress informal". Of course, I had not done this on my invitations and was therefore horrified, on the night of my dinner-party, to see two elderly couples walking up the path — the men in dinner-jackets and the women in long dresses. Of course we weathered it, and they were all very nice, but being in my very early thirties at the time I just wished the ground would open and swallow me up. However I learned and, acquiring a long skirt and a couple of tops, continued on my learning curve of do's and dont's when entertaining or being entertained at that period in Shropshire.

They were certainly very hospitable in Shropshire, and once I had learned how things were done, I enjoyed being entertained and indeed reciprocating the entertainment provided I had someone in the kitchen who could cook the main course. I could get ready the sweets and even the starters, but dishing up for a dinner party in a long skirt, in what still seemed the house next door but one, was really not on, so my entertaining tended to be spasmodic. But I felt strongly it had to be done — these people were sympathetic supporters of the school, many of them actual governors, and it was, I felt, important for them to meet the head in relaxed conditions and get the feel that the school was in good hands. Of course some were easier guests than others. The old bishop and his wife continued to be firm favourites, but among others, including some rather dour characters — of the kind who are always convinced that they alone are in the right — was a delightful peppering of mild eccentrics. I particularly remember the slight drama of going out to dinner with the vice-chairman of the governors, who to me was the quintessence of the eccentric Shropshire squire one might have found a century before. He was an erudite man with a library of books which he had obviously read, but the room where they were kept had a ceiling looking as if it would come down any moment — it was in fact held up by two high step-ladders with piles of cushions on top which supported the sagging ceiling. The night we were bidden to dinner was a warm airless one in late summer, and as we advanced towards the manor house through a pair of rusty gates, one actually hanging off its hinges, a thunderstorm broke making one feel one was somehow taking part in a film of an Emily Brontë book. A bumpy ride down a long drive rutted and full of potholes brought us to what had obviously been a very handsome 18th-century house, but now with peeling paint and some windows completely obscured by ivy it was not looking its best, and one felt the door might indeed be opened by Miss

Havisham. It seemed a long time before our hammering on the door (when we tried to pull the rusty bell-pull it had come away in my hand) was answered, but eventually our charming friendly hostess arrived surrounded by what seemed a great selection of dogs all barking furiously. (At least I was relieved to find that despite the prognostications of a waggish friend there did not appear to be any horses actually in the house.) A long walk down numerous passages full of "things" apparently wrapped in old curtains and past numerous closed doors brought us finally to a door which she opened to reveal astonishingly an exceptionally charming drawing-room.

It was high and well-proportioned with a beautifully-moulded ceiling and was full of lovely if shabby pieces of furniture, and from one of the comfortable if sagging chairs rose our host, delightfully attired in a white cricket shirt with a bootlace for a tie, a Centaurs' blazer and a pair of Yeomanry Blues trousers which had a large moth-hole in them just below one knee, which I found exceedingly difficult not to stare at. It was altogether a surprising evening. I remember excellent sherry and very fine wines perhaps not quite matched by a curious meal — the pheasant was certainly "higher" than most people find palatable, and through it all fascinating conversation — our host was quite an expert on Shropshire history and indeed many other things. But the surrealism was really made even more acute when in the middle of dinner there was a particularly vivid flash of lightning followed by a crash and all the lights went out. We finished our dinner

149

happily by the light of candles in magnificent solid silver candlesticks, but a problem arose when I was asked if I would like to "powder my nose". My hostess guided me to the bathroom which was a symphony of mahogany and brass, no doubt put in by a particularly "with-it" squire of the 19th century, but the problem was finding my way back by the light of a flickering candle. Having explored several passages I had to my shame to resort to calling out, "Please, I'm lost", whereupon my very kind hostess rescued me. But it was certainly an evening to remember, and very importantly the men developed a rapport which lasted all the time we were at Newport.

But of course to be what I envisaged as a "link-man" between the school and local people one had obviously to do a good deal more than go out to tea with local ladies and dine with local worthies. I realised very soon that I must be expected to join in all manner of local activities, whether or not they would normally be my choice.

The first of such activities that came my way was at least one in which I had a little experience. My elder daughter had started at the very good local "Dames' School" when we had moved to Newport, and among the parents with whom I became friendly was a very delightful farmer's wife who, as well as having a daughter at the Dames' School, also had three sons at the grammar school. She was a veritable pillar of society being a J.P. and connected with a great many organisations in the county including the Women's Institute. She was in fact president of the institute in her village, and also on the county committee. It so happened that the secretary of her particular institute had arranged for someone to come to the next meeting to speak on drama. This had all sounded quite interesting and acceptable to members until it became known that the speaker would need a "guinea pig" who would be willing to take part with the speaker in acting out short extracts from various scenes. Members were horrified. None of them had ever acted before, and none were certainly prepared to offer themselves as guinea pigs. My friend Molly knew of my abiding interest in anything to do with the theatre, so, as we waited one afternoon for our children to come out of school, she asked me whether I would be prepared to help by becoming a "temporary member" for this particular meeting and take on the dreaded role of "guinea pig", adding of course that if afterwards I would like to join as a proper member they would be delighted to have me — and she added persuasively that this sort of thing was very good for public relations. At first I was appalled at the thought of making a fool of myself in front of total strangers, but thinking it over, and knowing getting out into the community was obviously a good thing, I consented.

In actual fact it was rather fun. The other members were so grateful that I was getting them out of something they did not want to do, that they soon got over looking at me as if I was a visitor from outer space — and what I had to do for the speaker was simplicity itself. Noticing that I was obviously enjoying myself, Molly continued her persuasion. "Why don't you join our W.I. and start a little drama group? — They could do little sketches for our Christmas party, and I should be so grateful". "Well, why not?" I said cheerfully, and before I could change my mind Molly had announced the formation of the new drama group from the chair. Under the glow of enthusiasm radiated by the speaker, when possible members of this new group were called for, a number of the younger women put up their hands and said they would not mind, as long as it did not involve too much work. Hardly knowing what I was doing I suggested they came along to my house next week for a "sketch-reading" (I felt I could not quite dignify it with calling it a play-reading) and so began my involvement with at least one more branch of community life, which I think we all enjoyed.

The actual productions of the "Players Branch of the Lilleshall W.I." were not perhaps of great artistic merit, but they gave a great number of people a lot of fun. I had done quite a lot of acting but knew next to nothing about producing, so we all learned together. Initially, I threw myself on the tender mercies of our charming senior English master, who fortunately lived in the boarding house, and having laughed uproariously at the idea of the whole project he proceeded to be extremely helpful. He taught me the bare bones of how to prepare a producer's script and a producer's schedule, and followed this with invaluable advice about possible sketches. So a mere two weeks after my initial arrival on the scene of Lilleshall W.I., with the help of John White, the English master, the British Drama League and the county library, I nerved myself to meet my little group with what I hoped was at least a possible sketch which would do for the Christmas party, thankfully still some months away.

Five aspiring actresses turned up for the first reading. Fortunately I had chosen a sketch with only five characters — of whom really only three had real "acting" parts. This turned out to be just as well as of the five one delightful lady had really only come because she supported literally anything the W.I. chose to do, though she admitted cheerfully she "wasn't much good at this sort of thing and was not a bit of good at lines like". However, she was utterly content to turn up every week to say, "The car's at the door, Miss," with great aplomb though not always quite in the right place — but that was easy: on the night I was at hand to give her a shove at the appropriate moment. She was also splendid about collecting props. Her daughter, a very decorative girl, moved nicely and looked charming, and if it was hard to hear what she said beyond the third row, nothing she had to say was really of enormous importance to the plot and she certainly added a nice bit of glamour. The other three were really quite good and threw themselves wholeheartedly into the play whose plot concerned the mysterious disappearance of small objects from people's houses all over a village — who could be the culprit? As none of them had ever acted before my fine ideas of production and "letting them feel their way into their parts" somewhat went by the board, and I used to be asked, "How did you say that bit, dear?" as they tried to copy my inflections (I have to admit I tended to give them some idea of how

153

to say their lines), but we had fun and they really were not at all bad. And when it came to choosing dresses for the play they were as excited as small children, particularly the woman who was playing the *femme fatale*. Though my chief memory of dressing her was of her down-to-earth voice saying to me as I tried to get her into her modish dress with a bit of a struggle, "It's no good pushing me in there, dear. I mean to say what goes in one place is bound to stick out somewhere else, isn't it?"

Another more serious worry however as far as I was concerned was lighting and effects. Mercifully someone's kind husband volunteered to turn lights on and off at appropriate moments — we were not looking for subtle lighting, but what really worried me was that the sound of a car starting up, and also the screeching of brakes off-stage were very essential to the plot. Once more I turned to John White who cheerfully volunteered to produce a tape of the noises of cars starting and stopping with a squeal of brakes. And indeed the following weekend he and a colleague spent a considerable time driving their cars round the playground to the great amusement of the boys. What it did to their tyres I shudder to think, but certainly the noise played back to me on the tape was most effective.

By this time enthusiasm for the play was beginning to grip all the boarding masters, and the young art master offered to get one of his forms to produce some really splendid posters of varying degrees of luridness which when placed round the village gave great satisfaction to the players. Even Robert joined in the fun. "What about programme?" he said. And with the aid of the children's Bulldog printing set produced some splendid programmes which were then duplicated, even decorated with red holly berries, which were greatly admired. Finally the day of performance arrived and, loading our ancient car with quite a lot of our furniture for use on the stage, I prepared to set off for the village of Lilleshall with, I admit, more butterflies in my stomach than I normally have for even my own performance. Should I let them down? So much could go wrong. At the dress rehearsal for instance my *femme fatale* had forgotten almost half her lines, "It is the acting that does it, dear, I can't both act AND remember", and one of the others thought she was losing her voice. At the last minute, as promised John White turned up with the tape of the car starting, and a machine to play it on — on which I had practised assiduously, and also, surprisingly, a large balloon. "Double insurance," he announced laconically. "If for any reason the tape lets you down, try this" — and with that he drew his finger along the balloon thus producing a positively horrendous screeching sound, which could well be taken for the screech of car brakes.

At the village hall willing hands helped me to unload the car and we dressed the stage, and I walked the cast round it. There had been no chance of their rehearsing on stage with furniture in place before this, as at that time of the year a village hall is booked solid every afternoon and evening. All at once members of the institute and their friends and families began to arrive and the party began. It had been arranged that there should be carols, some games, a soloist, more carols, supper, and then what was expected to be the *pièce de résistance* of the evening — our play. At a suitable time before we were due to perform, I removed my cast from the festivities and began to do their make-up which they much enjoyed — except I had a small problem with the young woman who was supposed to be playing a seventy-year-old. Every time I put on a line she tended to rub it off, "I don't want to look TOO old — my husband would not like it." Someone else was clutching a VERY wet text: "I had it propped on the taps while I did the wash and of course it dropped in."

Finally the play got under way, and if it was not a very good production we got by and it was much enjoyed. The entrance of our "siren" occasioned quite a sensation, one heard little murmurs of "Coo, that's never Joyce." But the high spot of the evening was undoubtedly the effect caused by our screech of brakes. I had turned on the tape at the right moment for the starting of the car, and then almost immediately the tape seemed to die, and there was nothing. Grasping my balloon I drew my wetted finger across its surface as I had been told to do, and was rewarded by a most satisfactory piercing screech. There was a second's electric silence and then from the back of the hall a local farmer was heard to rise and rush out murmuring, "Oh Lord, I left my car in the road without any lights." Great hilarity followed and the evening was made.

As long as Robert was at Newport I continued to get great enjoyment from Lilleshall W.I. The annual sketch at the Christmas party became an institution, and over the years became slightly more professional. More members joined; husbands were cajoled into making bits of scenery, and to my great joy someone's son volunteered to take over the lights, so that in our last production we could actually show a change of light between morning and late evening. But we never lost the spirit of light-hearted camaraderie, and enjoyed each other's company. Meanwhile with all the Lilleshall friends I was making, I had no hesitation in joining the W.I. as a full member, learning incidentally a lot of useful skills like bread-making which a number of us learned actually in Molly's kitchen under the expert eye of a teacher of domestic science. This last activity was much approved of by my family. Finally I even took on the job of secretary of the little institute, and learned all the perils of arranging trips — when twenty people put their names down, and at the last moment only ten say they can come. On one occasion, when the trip was to a local zoo, I actually filled in with some junior boys from our boarding house, which made an odd but entirely happy combination. When we finally left Newport, Lilleshall W.I. presented me with two books about the countryside which I still treasure, and in presenting them to me, Molly made the point of saying how nice it was for them to have this link with the local grammar school that they were all so proud of. I had not consciously thought of it in that way, but looking back I suppose that was one of my first "link-man" efforts.

One little offshoot from my efforts with Lilleshall W.I. and doubtless as a direct result of kind words about me uttered by my friend Molly, I was invited to join the county drama committee of the W.I. where I endeavoured to do my little bit towards the production of a large pageant they were arranging to be presented in front of the late Princess Mary. I cannot pretend my membership of that committee was an unqualified success. I was certainly extremely frightened of most of the other members of the committee who were all much older and obviously knew each other very well. I still blush when I think of the occasion when they decided to change the venue for the next meeting, and knowing I did not know Shrewsbury very well, one of them asked me kindly if I knew how to find it. "Oh, yes," I said airily, "it is in the same road as my dentist." "Really," came the reply, "who is your dentist?" At that point my mind went entirely blank and there was a deathly silence while I struggled to get the name — and couldn't. They were kind about it but they looked at me a little warily, wondering no doubt what sort of addition they had got to their committee.

However I am pleased to say I did make one notable contribution to that pageant. It was to take the form of a sort of glorified card game with members dressed up to represent every card in the pack. Four "callers", armed with microphones, were then dealt "hands" and a game of whist proceeded with the callers calling out when their various cards were to move. Skilful

158

needlewomen, which did not, alas, include me, pronounced that the making of the costumes would cause "no problem", but were exercised by the fact that certainly all spades and clubs must wear black stockings. Where were they to get them? It was before black stockings suddenly made a reappearance and suddenly all the young were wearing them. We were sent away to think. However it so happened that in Newport there was a charming old-fashioned drapers run by two old sisters, so I went in and asked them if by any chance they had any black stockings stored away. Great consultations went on and then one of them apparently went up to an attic and returned with two dozen pairs, which I was invited to buy at a shilling a pair. Triumphantly I rang up my chairman and was authorised to buy the entire stock, and when I arrived at the next committee meeting clutching my precious haul I was given a hero's welcome.

A totally unforeseen result of my joining Lilleshall W.I. as their dramatic guinea-pig, that fateful afternoon, was my introduction into public speaking — which incidentally can come in handy for any headmaster's wife who inevitably gets asked from time to time to open this or that or judge this or that. At that time Shropshire W.I., under the leadership of no other a person than Lady Denman, was particularly progressive, and it so happened that it had been decided that W.I. members should be encouraged to be able to "say a few words" if asked, at least audibly and to the point. It had therefore been decided to hold a competition between all the willing W.I.s in which three members would "say a few words". For some reason it was decided that one of the "team" must do a book-review, and needless to say Lilleshall decided unanimously that that would be my role. Slightly bemused I said I would have a go, and chose as my book to be reviewed *Lark Rise to Candleford*. It did not have to last more than ten minutes at the outside. With some trepidation I worked on my little speech, and then inevitably on the day that the judges were coming to our area I went down with flu. At this point there was really no-one who could take over my slot, so having spent the day in bed, I got up in the evening and Robert drove me to the hall where it was to take place.

I remember very little about that evening. Luckily I had worked hard on my little speech, and learned it by heart, and when I was literally pushed on stage at the appropriate moment my automatic pilot must have taken over. Apparently I got through it without a hitch, and having finished it was driven home to bed, where a solicitous Robert discovered I had a temperature of 104. However I suffered no permanent ill-effects, and my "team" scored high enough to be asked to send a member to take part in a competition for W.I. speaker of the year for Shropshire. To my horror Lilleshall were unanimous in sending me. This time we were allowed to choose our own subject and I chose, as the subject to speak on for ten minutes, my formidable but fascinating Scottish grandmother. I did not win the little silver cup — quite rightly a speaker who talked knowledgably and delightfully about old Shropshire

160

customs got that, but I was adjudged second, which pleased my friends at Lilleshall enormously and at least gave me some useful experience for the inevitable requests to "say a few words" as I began to get further out and about.

CHAPTER
ELEVEN

Further out and about

I had made a small start with my activities with Lilleshall W.I. to send out a signal that the new regime was only too happy to do anything they could to help in the community, and after that requests to undertake more public commitments followed thick and fast. There is always a shortage of people in any small community to open fêtes, judge baby shows, and even serve upon brains trusts, so the appearance of a new sucker prepared to do these things was hailed with relief, whether the new guinea-pig was very good at any of these things or not. I remember very clearly the first time someone asked me to open a fête in a village near Newport, demurring desperately, saying, "I am sure you can find someone better than me", to be told in effect, though with great politeness, "Well, no, actually, we've had every one of real importance and now are down to you."

Over the 23 years as headmaster's wife at Newport, then at Monmouth, I certainly opened at least one fête or Christmas fair every year, and I hope I got better at it. The very first one I opened was a very small affair in a tiny village just outside Newport — though from the "nerves" I suffered one might have thought I was going to make a speech in the Albert Hall, as I wrote and re-wrote my little speech. But small though it was I learned some useful tips. As I worked my way through the speech, not helped by the peculiar public address system which made my voice sound as if it was actually a rival concern coming from the field next door but one, I realised that no-one was listening. They were in fact all intent on studying what was on the surrounding stalls in the peacefulness of everyone (except me) being quiet, and having decided what they wanted to go for, could hardly wait for me to finish so that they could get to the coveted prize before their neighbours. So I learned that to be a popular opener, you should just say how beautiful the stalls look (which is a safe bet), how hard everyone must have worked (which is bound to be true), and how worthy the cause is (having made sure you know what it is) and then bring one's "few words" to a rapid close, and get on with what one has really been brought there to do, namely go round buying lavishly from every stall, avoiding of course those things on which Mrs Smith or Mrs Jones has by now rapidly put "sold" labels. Only once did this tried and tested formula almost let me down, when I realised as I went on that I had forgotten to ask the vicar my usual question about what was the main object for the money raised. Turning to the vicar I asked the question, and had my ingenuity tested as to how to bring this graciously into my speech when he replied, "Oh, it's for the toilets in the church hall, the old ones are really shocking." I managed to say something about "improved amenities", and was rewarded at the end by the little Welsh vicar coming up to me beaming and saying, "Improved amenities. Yes, that was very nicely put."

Apart from that, two fêtes or fairs stand out in my memory, both near Monmouth. On the occasion of the first of these in a small nearby town, having arrived at the vicarage, I was driven through streets to the venue of the fête in a superb vintage car, with my chauffeur dressed in Edwardian costume. I felt very regal as I returned the waves of the crowd, though I was somewhat brought down to earth when I heard a youngster saying to his friend, "Smashing car, mind. But what's she doing inside it?"

My second vivid memory is of a Christmas fair in a small Welsh mining town. I had been warned by the vicar, whom I knew well, as he had been a former curate at Monmouth, "The public address system is awful, but you will have to use it or you won't be heard at all. They mean no harm, but they simply will not stop talking." He was certainly right about the public address system I realised as I listened to it squeaking and puffing as the Vicar shouted through it in his opening remarks. So when my turn came, I firmly refused it and advancing to the front of the stage roared in a stentorian voice (having done some acting helps on these occasions), "How about a little bit of hush?" There was a moment's startled silence as everyone stared at this eccentric lady in a hat behaving like this, and before the hubbub started again I said in my normal voice, "Look, I've come thirty miles to see you and spent quite a time thinking of nice things to say about you, and you are jolly well going to hear them — I promise I'll keep it short." Immediately I was answered by a voice coming from the back saying, "Quite right girl" and a great guffaw of laughter. I kept it short and they more or less listened, interpolating their own comments as we went along, so that it began to feel like a glorified cross-talk act. But I had the best "hand" I have ever had and they could not have been nicer to me as I did my round of the stalls. "Any chocolate cakes left?" I asked hopefully at the cake stall; Robert was very fond of chocolate cake. "Sorry, love," said a large lady beside me, "I think they have all gone — but look — the one I've bought is a real whopper, so I'll cut it down the middle and we'll have half each," which is what we did.

Certainly that little community was very welcoming — unlike in another fête, where when I arrived in what I considered to be "good time" I was greeted by the vicar saying, "Oh, whatever am I going to do with you — the opening isn't for ten minutes." To which I found myself answering a little wearily, "Just shove me in a corner until you are ready. I won't run away" — which is what happened.

Judging baby shows, another occupational hazard for a headmaster's wife trying to do her job in the community, is that it carries the risk that people do remember what you said, and the mothers of unsuccessful candidates can hold it against you for months afterwards. The first one I got roped in for was run by the Newport Rugby Club, as part of their fête.

Seemingly endless rows of healthy scrubbed youngsters were displayed for my inspection, and the task was obviously going to be very difficult indeed. However I concentrated on the babies, to the exclusion of the mothers holding them, which perhaps was a mistake and eventually found my winner, a lovely little boy, not too fat, but lively and glowing with health and intelligence. As the announcement was made, I thought the clapping seemed rather perfunctory, certainly no more than polite, and as I turned away a strapping young woman holding one of the podgiest babies stood in my path. "I can't think where your eyes are," she almost shouted at me. "My Carol's won the baby shows at three fêtes round here in the last month." As I was creeping away I bumped into the rector's wife on her way to judge the flower arrangement. "Been doing the babies?" she asked. "Dreadful job. I have refused to do it for the last ten years, said I was too old. Last time I did it hardly anyone came to church for a couple of months. I suppose you gave it to either the Griffiths or the Jones baby. It does not matter too much which — they are related." "No," I said, "I gave it someone called Pyner." Mrs Bradley looked horrified. "Good Heavens," she exclaimed. "Now you really have put the cat among the pigeons — they certainly would not be considered locally to qualify — they have only been here a year. Someone from the Griffiths family or Jones family or at a pinch the Harrison family always wins it. I should have told you. Never mind — I'm sure you will live it down." I did — eventually and at least no-one ever asked me to judge a baby show in Newport again, and

I resolved, when we went to Monmouth, that if I was ever asked I would have a very pressing engagement at the other side of the county that day.

Brains trusts were another section of public appearances for which locally well-known, but not too important, people such as headmasters' wives are considered to qualify. Invariably of course, if it was known I was on the panel, questions about corporal punishment would come up. However, carefully briefed by Robert, I got used to coping with the loaded wording in which these questions were often phrased. Usually I survived these functions without making a complete fool of myself, if not with distinction, except on one occasion when I was asked to sit on a panel run by the local branch of the Young Farmers, when I was completely out of my depth. "Interesting lot of questions," the burly question master informed me, when I arrived. "A bit technical but some interesting subjects." I was horrified. "You do know I know absolutely nothing about farming," I interposed nervously. He looked at me over his glasses. "But you are a farmer's daughter, aren't you?" he asked. "That is why we asked you." "NO," I wailed, "I was brought up in a cathedral city and have lived in cities all my life." He looked appalled, "Well, you had better sit next to me," he said, "and if there is a question you feel you can cope with give me a nudge and I will let you go first, before I give it to the experts, you know — woman's point of view — then perhaps they won't notice you don't answer the farming questions." On the whole this worked. Predictably I aired my views on corporal punishment, once again, and did my best with the National Health system and even environmental controls. But I got really landed once when there was a question on egg production and when I sneezed at the same time as the question was asked, the chairman thought I had nudged him. It would have been better if even at this point I had said I did not want to speak on this, but foolishly I mumbled away on what I thought I had heard other people say on the subject and got completely torn to shreds by the next speaker. As I left the meeting an old farmer came up to me and said with a grin, "Nice to have you with us but you don't know much about farming do you?"

However whether I fulfilled these obligations efficiently or in a thoroughly half-baked manner, it seemed I was given points for trying. After all a willing horse is a handy thing to have about the place, and obviously my being ready to come out from the fastnesses of the school environment to do what I could was appreciated. Which, after all was the object of the exercise. So when in our last year at Newport it was decided that Newport would be a good place to have a branch of the Townswomen's Guild, I suppose it seemed a sensible thing for the powers that be to approach me to be its founder chairman, as it was pointed out that I was able to represent the interests of both sides of the little town.

I knew absolutely nothing about the organisation at this time, but said I would have a try, which is why I did a lot of things — I could not think of a good reason to say "No" and it could be good for public relations.

Newport was an expanding little town at the time, and quite a number of women of all ages came along to the inaugural meeting. A steering committee was elected and there seemed to be quite a lot of enthusiasm for the whole concept. There was one moment when I wondered if the whole conception was going to founder on some T.W.G. red tape, but luckily fate was on our side. The officials had told me that, according to the rules, before a new branch can be recognised officially the constitution and rules must be read to the members in the presence of the regional officials — and my committee were very worried. "It will turn all the young ones away," they said. "They don't want to spend an evening listening to rules." However on the evening when it should have happened there was a tremendous fall of snow between Shrewsbury and Newport, though not in Newport itself, and the regional officials rang me to say they could not get through, and the reading of the rules would have to be postponed. However, at this point I saw my chance to let us off the hook. I asked whether in these circumstances I, as founder president, might not stand in for them in their official capacity — and after some demurring permission was given. So, while the secretary got down to finding someone willing to show slides of an interesting summer holiday, I settled down to some rapid précis writing, and when the time came, the reading of the rules and constitution, which the officials told me would take over half an hour, had been contracted to ten minutes and I felt that everyone understood the basics perfectly well — and we got on with our really rather good slides and a discussion of some of the cities of Eastern Europe. At all events that particular branch of the Townswomen's Guild, despite its unorthodox beginnings, certainly flourished and continued, I am glad to say, to flourish ten years later, and again forty years later I was asked back to their celebration dinner, and was delighted to see how it had grown and how lively it was.

When we arrived at Monmouth where the town-and-gown relationships were not nearly so comfortable, I had hoped that by joining the well-established Townswomen's Guild there, that too might be a help in making clear the principle that people such as myself so intimately connected with the school were only too delighted to join in whatever was going on in the town. My experiences, here, however were even from the beginning not nearly so comfortable. At first it looked as if my entrée into the branch would be simple, as it so happened that for some reason they had decided to produce a pageant on cotton through the ages and were looking for any help they could get, and the nice wife of one of Robert's colleagues, who was on the committee, knowing that I was both a historian of sorts, and certainly devoted to drama, thought it would be a splendid idea if I actually wrote the scenario of the pageant for them — and took me along to a committee meeting. I thought I got a somewhat luke-warm reception from the "management" — I suppose they thought of me as an outsider trying to muscle in, but they graciously permitted me at least to "have a go".

170

I really rather enjoyed researching and writing that pageant — something I had never tried before. It had ten scenes starting with the Egyptians, and worked its way through the crusades, the court of Elizabeth, South American cotton, the Industrial Revolution and goodness knows what else to the present day. So I typed it all out with my two-finger typing and took it along to the president, hoping for a kindly reception. However a week later I was summoned to a meeting at the president's house where I was told my pageant really would not do — it was too long and most of it was unsuitable. They might use a page or two out of an odd scene, but even that would have to be changed out of existence. In considerable disappointment I returned home with my tail between my legs. It had not even been suggested that I should help in any way.

Four months later I read in the local paper that a pageant on cotton written by the president herself was to be produced. "I should not go," Robert counselled wisely — but of course I could not resist it. I have seldom been so angry in my life. Before my astonished eyes MY pageant, with only the most minor alterations unfolded before me, under the president's name and with no reference to me at all. I sat there unbelieving as people round me told each other what a delightful concept it all was, and so well-written, and at the end I rushed from the hall without speaking to anyone. Robert listened sympathetically but then said extremely firmly, "There is nothing you can do. No-one but the president had been allowed to read your script and it is her word against yours. You are not known, and she is

171

— and with us only just moving here it will do nothing but harm to town-and-gown relations if you have a public row. Forget it." I could not, of course, and after all these years the memory still rankles, but he was no doubt right. What I did realise however very clearly was that this was not going to be my bridge into good relations with the community — I must find something else.

The bridge, when I finally found it, came via a very unexpected source — the Girl Guide movement. Through the post one morning I received an invitation to an annual general meeting of the local branch of Girl Guides, so I went along. It was quite a small meeting, and everyone was obviously astonished to see me, but they made me very welcome. During the course of the meeting, one of the local Guide captains, a local vicar's wife, asked for a volunteer to give her some help for a few months. Apparently her daughter was getting married, and understandably she was going to be very busy and would very much appreciate a stand-in who could take weekly meetings when she was involved with her preparations. Well, I had been a Girl Guide in my far-off schooldays, and had even been a Ranger and a Company Leader, so, in the tea-interval I went along to see Mrs Lewis, the Guide captain who had asked for help, and offered my services, such as they were. I was met with the, by now, expected response — blank astonishment from Mrs Lewis. "You would not want to do that," she said. "On the contrary, I should be only too willing, if I can be of any help at all," I replied. And so I was received into the fold. Robert thought it was hilarious, but agreed I had done the right thing, but my two daughters, now thirteen and eleven were tremendously impressed — they were Girl Guides themselves by now in a different company — and consumed with envy for my officer's uniform. So in the next few weeks I went on a refresher course in a beautiful house in Wales, and learned just how much I had forgotten — and how odd it was to be sleeping in a dormitory again. At home I spent a lot of time re-learning my knots and the Guide Law, coached by Kate and Jane. And on each Tuesday for the next six months I quite enjoyed myself taking the little meeting!

During that summer my little company had two high spots. One was the opportunity to take part in a county pageant — I seemed to be dogged by pageants, but at least this one has nothing but pleasant associations. The other was their annual camp. In the pageant, which was designed to illustrate all the activities in which Girl Guides participate, our "spot" was to portray a country ramble. It was to take place on Chepstow race course, so there was no question of speech — whatever we did had to be portrayed in mime. We decided we would mime reading a compass, picking and identifying wild flowers, listening to bird-song, and as a "climax" having a meal round a camp-fire. How to produce a "lookalike" fire in a few seconds — there was obviously no possibility of having a real fire in the middle of a racecourse — would obviously need some ingenuity, so I consulted our senior science master, who came up with a magical solution. Producing two small bottles, he demonstrated that if they were held neck to neck with their stoppers out, some most realistic "smoke" would result. So, on the day, while the younger Guides carried a selection of twigs, the oldest and most reliable Guide carried the two magic bottles, in a container masked by more pieces of wood. Then when the others had laid the fire, at the appropriate moment she bent over the collection of twigs, and removed the stoppers in the bottles for a few seconds. The resulting "Ooh" from the audience, gave them tremendous satisfaction, and having apparently fried some sausages — and certainly eaten them, they then removed themselves from the racecourse without leaving a trace, and were thrilled to get some very nice words of commendation from the commentator at the microphone who was explaining to the audience what was going on.

The other high spot of that summer, the annual camp held in a field some miles from Monmouth, held for me, I have to say, a certain quality of ordeal. Of course I had camped in my youth, but I was beginning to feel that was a very long time ago. Needless to say there were the usual mosquitoes, without which, in my experience, no camp is complete; needless to say there was a bull in the field between our camp and the little church where we were to go for church parade; needless to say I was put in charge of the latrines; and needless to say there was such a rainstorm one night that one tent was completely flooded out, and we had to mount a rescue operation at three o'clock one morning. However I was saved from the worst of the discomforts of trying to sleep on a straw palliasse. When I bemoaned the fact that nowadays I should

174

never manage to sleep on a palliasse, Robert said firmly, "In that case I should not try — take along the camp-bed I had in the army — you will sleep all right on that." When I protested it would not look right, he laughed me to scorn. "The art of soldiering is to make yourself as comfortable as you can in the most unlikely situations and I don't see why Girl Guides should be any different. If you had not got an available camp-bed, fair enough — you would have to put up with it. But you have — so for goodness sake use it. You will be far more use to everyone if you have had a decent night's sleep." So, rather sheepishly, I took the little bed along, to be met, as I had expected, with some scorn from the other officers from other companies who were sharing our camp. However next morning when in answer to a number of rather sour enquiries about how I had slept, I answered I had slept like a top, there were a number of telephone calls made from the box down the road, and when visiting day came two days later, I did not fail to observe that three husbands of other officers arrived clutching camp-beds.

My Guiding only lasted six months, but it did prove to be the bridge between me and the community, for once it became known that this new headmaster's wife was really willing to come out of the ivory tower of Monmouth School and join in life in the town, the invitations began to arrive inviting me to join in whatever was going on. For instance another vicar's wife, hearing from Mrs Lewis about my helping with the Guides, asked me if I would come along to her Mothers' Union to give a "little talk". I felt I could not

175

refuse this invitation to join in the activities of the community, but I admit I was frankly horrified at the thought of talking to a Mothers' Union meeting. What could I talk about? Would they expect a message? "Oh, no dear," said the Vicar's wife kindly. "You will be the light relief." So, as I had done when asked to speak on behalf of my branch of the W.I. in Shropshire, out came my little talk on my lively Scottish grandmother, who again was kindly received. And during the next years, Granny and I proceeded to tour Mothers' Unions, Church Guilds and Women's Bright Hours — and indeed all sorts of small organisations who were in need of a new speaker. It used to amuse me, as I left one of these meetings, how surprised Granny would be if she could have known how her little eccentricities had become the tea-and-biscuit topics of tiny halls over a remote part of England long after she was dead. Her refusal to have Sweet Williams in the house because they were named after the Duke of Cumberland (stinking billies she used to call them), her dislike of sopranos (those screeching women abuse a body's ears), and her down-to-earth approach to an auction room, which incidentally saved me many a pound — "a bargain isn't a bargain if you don't really want it" — still raised little smiles over thirty years after she had gone. To me she did a great service, for listening to me chatter about Granny, all sorts and conditions of people began to accept me, and I was asked to help with fund-raising efforts for all sorts of charities and when finally my tentative suggestion that they might like to hold a coffee-morning in my house was accepted I felt that a real bridge between the school and the local community was being built — beneficial I believed most strongly to both parties.

By the end of the second or third year at Monmouth I was beginning to feel that with my comic foray into the Girl Guides, my willingness to undertake to be a speaker, if inexpert, at small meetings, and my genuine interest in helping any charity committee, I was getting across my gospel that despite what might have happened before, those intimately connected with the school were genuinely concerned about local interests, and only too happy to fill any gaps they could. But there were three very diverse areas where I felt I could add my pennyworth towards the general well-being of the community.

The first of these was the Citizens' Advice Bureau. When I arrived in Monmouth the local Citizens' Advice Bureau was manned entirely by voluntary workers, drawn from every walk of life and run by an elderly colonel with efficiency and caring. However they were short of people who could give their time to it — so I offered my services. It was a very interesting experience, and I for one gained valuable insight into all manner of problems faced by local people about which I had had no idea. Of course we could not solve all the problems; some were frankly insoluble — a real clash of personalities will defy the most earnest efforts of the most dedicated worker — and some were frankly not meant to be solved. We had one delightful old lady who came in week after week with some quite impossible problem. We all talked seriously round it, and in the end got nowhere, but soon came to realise this didn't really matter. What the old lady enjoyed was the chat and someone taking an interest in her affairs, whether or not they could actually do much to alleviate the problem.

A second very different and, it might be thought, frivolous affair in which I involved myself was the founding of a lunch club, a mixed one for both men and women to meet once a month in one of Monmouth's hotels. Many years before when we were at Canterbury, I had attended such a club, which had been run by Mrs Shirley, the headmaster's wife at the time of King's School, Canterbury, and still remembered the tonic it had been for a young mother, very much buried under the ties of nappies and Farex to put on "tidy" clothes, eat a meal that someone else had cooked, and spend a pleasant hour or so listening to an interesting talk and conversing with pleasant strangers on all sorts of topics. Of course a lot of Jeremiahs said it would not work, and it had been tried before, but I threw a party for everyone I felt might be interested, and having got a nucleus went ahead and to my joy from a very small beginning it took off, and at the end of the first year had a membership of 100 and a waiting list of 80. We ran it on a shoestring — my children well remember being sent off on their bicycles to deliver monthly notices, to save the postage, but with so little spent on administration we could afford better speakers. I remember, for instance, with pleasure such diverse speakers as Lady Barnett, Godfrey Talbot, Brian Johnson (especially for Robert — or indeed all the sports-loving men), the Duke of Bedford and Arthur Negus to name only a few. Though of course some were more popular than others. I remember a very young man, now a well-known figure in the media, bringing a blush to the cheeks of some of our more elderly members by his language (I remember giving him a few gentle words on the subject when I said goodbye to him, which he took very well). I also remember a well-known speaker being unwise enough to talk down to a by-and-large intelligent audience, which went down badly. In contrast was the delightful, erudite and utterly charming manner of Neville Coghill. He spoke to the members about his London production of the *Canterbury Tales* as if we were all on his academic level. Or there were the times of course when the speaker passed muster but the lunch was not up to the standard some members felt it should be. Indeed I remember very well on one occasion when I was actually not there, being in bed with chickenpox of all undignified things, a member rang up to tell me her soup had been cold, and she hoped I would do something about it. But by and large the lunches were highly enjoyable occasions attended by a complete cross-section of the local community, including I was delighted to see, quite a few young mothers (some of our younger masters' wives), who like me in those far-off days were obviously enjoying a break from household chores. I am delighted to say that the enterprise continued to flourish after we had left, and indeed is still in good health, having earned a place in Monmouth life.

The third project in which I involved a large cross-section of the local community and the boys of the school was an annual event known as the Animal Fair, which took place at the end of the summer term. Quite early on in our time at Monmouth, I had become involved with a local committee whose aim was to give what help it could to the local Cheshire Home. I joined in the fund-raising events, and took my turn in going to the home once a fortnight to take home-baked tea to the residents, which was obviously appreciated. After a time, I persuaded the committee to allow me to take with me when I went three or four sixth form boys to bring another world to the residents and the experiment was an undoubted success. I obviously chose the boys carefully from volunteers, but I remembered so well how my father, who in old age became almost immobile with arthritis, always opted for my children to help him rather an adult because, as a proud man he found their help easier to accept, as he said they accepted his incapacity without pitying him. And so I saw it was again. The men in particular in the home welcomed these youngsters who could talk sport so much better than even the most dedicated member of the ladies' committee. It was also interesting to note that some of the boys who Robert said tended to break every rule in the book, were the most successful visitors, and writing references at the end of their time at school, Robert often said, "Thank God for the Cheshire Home — at least it gives me something positively nice to say about this difficult chap."

180

Driving home one afternoon with some of the boys, after we had been visiting our Cheshire Home, one of them asked me whether perhaps the school as a whole might do something to raise money for these people of whom they were getting very fond — perhaps through some sort of fête at the end of term. So to try and make it a slightly different event from the ordinary church fête, I came up with the idea of an animal fair, — a sort of glorified pet show with stalls and sideshows run by the boys. Robert gave his approval, and the idea went ahead. Of course there were problems, particularly as it obviously had to be after the end of term, when one could expect most boarders to have gone home, and many people told me it was "impossible". However the impossible has always had a certain attraction for me so we struggled on. The masters on the whole were very much in favour of the idea, as thinking out their stalls and sideshows gave boys in the difficult days when the exams are finished — and the devil seems to suggest to boys at these times, a whole range of illicit and interesting things to do — an interest and purpose.

In order to get in touch with pet-owners, I circularised every primary and secondary school in the area, and found the head teachers without exception wonderfully co-operative about publicising the event and handing out entrance-forms to pet-owners. I admit I was somewhat staggered by the variety of would-be entrants. I had said "All comers" and I certainly got them. Every conceivable variety of cat, dog and rabbit seemed to be represented, as well as ponies, hamsters, goldfish and birds — and even the odd goat, sheep and

181

cock and I particularly remember a baby salmon. Fortunately, not really knowing much about animals myself, I had a friend who knew a great deal, and who, in answer to my frantic phone call came along and took charge of the ever-growing motley list of entries, sorting them into possible classes. Two entries constituted a "class" as far as we were concerned and the "one-offs" simply had to go into a general class we called "unusual". It was Betty who early on raised the vital subject of judges. As she said, "No good bringing in the real experts here." In the end we settled for friendly farmers and a couple of my friends who I knew had a great love, a working knowledge and intelligent interest in animals. In fact I found a wonderful team of six who worked in pairs with only one change over the next ten years, who very kindly said that Animal Fair day was one of the most enjoyable days of their year. I remember particularly a large, friendly and exuberant farmer, much loved by the children, who would examine each hedgehog or hamster or whatever with such careful attention and scrutiny that the anxious owners knew their precious pet was receiving maximum attention. It was Jimmy in fact who, when we came to discuss rosettes for the winners, red for firsts, blue for seconds and yellow for thirds, suggested that we should also have another green rosette for "Special". He pointed out that if you have at least five or six entries in a class, the owners who do not win one of the prized rosettes can console each other, but if there were only four entries he could not bear to see one child standing left without one — after all every animal is "special" to its owner. The success of the fair owed a great deal to Jimmy who, when on one occasion the fair coincided with his having a party of weekend houseguests, simply brought them all along with instructions to go and try their luck at every sideshow — and so they did.

Meanwhile Betty continued to manage the animal side of things and raised the important question of where the animals were to go when they arrived. As she pointed out the ponies and dogs were all right — they could stay with their owners but how about the cats and rabbits and hamsters or white mice? However fortunately, having asked the question she answered it herself. "I have it," she said, "try the auctioneers."

The auctioneers were mildly surprised when I approached them but very co-operative and offered to let me have as many cages as I wanted free of charge, provided I fetched them and brought them back in time for the next market-day.

Meanwhile enthusiasm among the sideshows was growing. Several farmers' sons offered to bring along ponies, and give rides, while the sister of one of them, who actually ran a small riding-school, offered to bring along her quieter ponies — and needless to say on the afternoon they were busy the whole time. Another very practical farmer's son offered to bring along straw to put in the cages — for which I was very grateful, as I had not thought of that. Meanwhile the boys who were running a fascinating variety of sideshows had got themselves organised, and what is more had found their own prizes from parents, friends and friendly shopkeepers, and the local committee got down to the

183

business of supplying all comers with home-made cakes for tea.

I don't think I shall ever forget that first Animal Fair. The morning was spent rushing between school and playing field, which was the other side of the river, with all the things I had forgotten despite careful lists. Where were the receptacles for change, the bowls for water for thirsty animals, the jugs in which to mix the orange squash? Meanwhile the ground staff were working like Trojans, marking out judging rings, fetching benches and assembling the cages, which proved diabolical to do. Robert had driven our caravan down onto the field to act as an office, a focal point for recording entries, a place to house the prizes and rosettes, and act as a bank — and to my relief he himself offered to act as banker. Somehow to my surprise we were actually ready to receive the first entries.

In fact the first competitor arrived a good 30 minutes before "opening time" — a large ginger cat in the arms of a stolid flaxen-haired small girl, and was ceremoniously taken to his cage and given his number. And suddenly the place was alive with cars arriving full of seemingly hordes of children clutching every conceivable kind of pet, all very excited. Soon the caravan was surrounded with a seething mass of children carrying animals, but happily forming themselves into an orderly queue to be registered by the imperturbable Betty, and put into classes. I have a particularly happy memory of passing the queue at one point and seeing two children standing one behind the other, the front one holding the lead of a small

Dachshund and the one behind the lead of a Great Dane, looking down at his fellow competitor with benevolent interest, and the patient air of a habitué of a cinema queue. In all the twelve years I ran the Animal Fair we never had any trouble between the animals who seemed to have a sense of occasion — this was their day, and they behaved like responsible citizens. In fact the only recorded accident of any kind during those years was the nip which a hamster gave a judge, who was unwise enough to put his hand into the cage, as he recognised the hamster was one he had given to his godson and thought he was safe. But the hamster obviously felt this was not an occasion when liberties should be taken.

The afternoon wore on and excited owners began to appear leading animals with rosettes attached to their collars. The sideshows were doing great business, including one run by my son Richard, aged eight, and a friend, who made a great deal of money. In this case I was somewhat mystified what one actually had to do to get one's money back, as I suspect other people were, but nobody seemed to mind. Meanwhile his sisters were happily and stickily helping with the ice-cream stall. Suddenly about 4 o'clock it began to rain — which at least meant that everyone made a great rush to the tea-tent, which consequently did great business. On my way to see how this was going on I became aware of a small boy in T shirt and shorts happily bouncing on the trampoline. "It's raining," I called. "Put on your coat." "It's not," he replied laconically and continued to bounce.

Suddenly it was all over and we were left with an empty field and a satisfyingly large collection of wet coins which I found Robert counting imperturbably into bags as the stall-holders brought in their contributions. At this point I was called back to the entrance where a minibus containing the more mobile residents of Llanhennock Cheshire Home were about to go home, surrounded by boys who had so often visited them, and obviously having had a great day out. It was most satisfying. That night I was so tired I thought I could never face organising another such fair — but of course I did. I doubt if either the Llanhennock residents or, even more, local pet-owners would have let me give it up. At the beginning of each successive summer I would be stopped in the town by anxious pet-owners telling me how they were busy grooming Topsy or training Rover — and there would be another Animal Fair wouldn't there. So it continued until we left — and I got better at the organisation. There is no doubt it proved a particularly happy link between the school, the town, and the surrounding villages whose little schools sent in a progressively large number of hopeful applicants.

CHAPTER
TWELVE

A safe pair of hands

In her role of residuary legatee then, the headmaster's wife may find herself coping with such things as catering (which may in times of crisis include cooking for numbers) and acting as matron, whether she is qualified to do so or not. She will also certainly be expected to entertain a wide variety of people in her home, from the immediate school "family" of staff, boys, parents and governors, to visitors of every description who come to the school. She must also very importantly act as the "link-man" between the school and the local community, so that the school is never seen to be aloof or stand-offish. But apart from these things, which become part of a pleasant varied routine, she must be prepared to provide a safe pair of hands ready to cope with any crisis large or small which may from time to time occur in the school. Over the years I got to know that particular look on Robert's face as he came through to the house from his study, with a seemingly particularly heavy tread, and uttered those words, full of foreboding, "We have a crisis". Some were comparatively trivial, some I was more qualified to cope with than others, but it was understood perfectly between us that until a real solution could be found to solve that crisis I must do my best to fill the gap.

Of course, in my own true sphere of action at Newport, the kitchen, I was forever dealing with crises — often of my own making. Such was the time when in my inexperience I ordered far too much cabbage, and to save my face had to pretend it was all done to provide the boys with a particularly nutritious soup. I spent hours making that soup, whose recipe indeed had taken a great deal of research, and the boys thoroughly enjoyed it and were always asking if they could have it again. I am afraid they never got it. Or there was the time — not my fault on this occasion — when the local farmer delivering a vast quantity of eggs, slipped on the newly washed kitchen floor and nearly every egg was smashed — whereupon cook had hysterics. I remember saying as calmly as I could, "Well, scrambled eggs for boys' supper tonight". But these crises, though very real to me, did not affect the school in general. Even the very boring fortnight when I spent an unconscionable time sewing on buttons because the sewing woman was ill was hardly worth a mention over the supper table. However the time when Robert was without a secretary for three weeks because the current one left somewhat suddenly and no suitable replacement could be found at short notice was of much greater significance. I managed to discover that the groundsman's wife could do a little typing — though I have to say her spelling nearly gave Robert a stroke — and I myself manned the telephone. But when Robert came through and said firmly, "The groundsman's wife cannot possibly do the wages", I admit I was appalled. "I am afraid there is no-one else so . . ." said Robert and left. I threw myself on the mercy of the senior mathematics master who initiated me into the intricacies of P.A.Y.E. and insurances, and for a dizzy three weeks I think I actually understood them, but I was more than overjoyed to hand it all over into the competent hands of the new secretary when she arrived.

Crises concerning masters were of course nothing to do with me — except on three occasions. The first of these Robert actually knew nothing about. One evening, when Robert was out at a meeting, my front door bell went and I found a young master standing there looking both worried and sheepish. "I wonder if you can help me," he said. "I don't know who else to go to." I asked him in and it emerged that he had been to a party and though he was by no means drunk, was worried that perhaps he had had too much to drink to drive home safely. I sat him down and filled him with black coffee and made a great dish of scrambled egg (of course he had had nothing to eat) and at the end of an hour we both decided he was by now perfectly all right to drive the mile home. Next day a delicious box of chocolates arrived from him. "What is all this about?" said Robert. "Oh, he had some problem over his car and I was able to find some help," I said airily. "Decent of him," said Robert — and no more was said.

Another crisis connected with the masters was far more demanding. One morning one of the masters whose wife we all knew was expecting her third baby rang in a state of great agitation. Apparently the baby

189

had arrived in the night three weeks early, and nothing was ready and the relative who was expected to help could not come yet. All was confusion and he did not know when he could get to school. On getting the message Robert came through to the house and told me, and then just looked at me. "All right," I said, "I'll go", and went off on my bicycle. As I arrived at the house the district nurse was just leaving. "How is everything?" I enquired anxiously. "Mother and baby are fine," she answered. "No problem there. But the rest of the house is chaos and old night. If you have come to help, the best of British luck", and off she cycled.

As I walked up the path I could see our scholarly young master standing by the sink, looking helplessly at a pile of after-birth washing, while his two young sons, aged four and two respectively, clamoured round him, one demanding something to eat, and the other asking him to mend his toy motor car. "I've come to help," I said brightly. "What can I most usefully do?" He smiled at me a little wanly. "How very kind," he said. "Perhaps you could look after these two for a little while so that I can do something about this . . ." His voice trailed away as he looked again at the pile of soiled bed-linen waiting to be washed. The two small boys, whom I hardly knew, looked at me with some alarm. After all their little world had been turned upside down, and what they needed was Daddy, not some strange woman, however well-intentioned. So, "No," I said firmly. "You cope with your children and I'll cope with the washing. I'm more used to it than you are." The

190

look of relief on his face was almost comical and he vanished at speed into the garden, leaving me gazing at that unattractive mound of washing. There was no washing-machine, and, seemingly little hot water in the taps. However I found the soap powder and boiled kettles, and feeling very much in the tradition of Florence Nightingale (the strongest of you are wanted in the wash tub) I plunged into my self-appointed task. I don't know how long it took me — I seemed to be washing for ever but at last all was clean and on the line, and having seen mother and baby had all they wanted I cycled a little wearily home. Mercifully my help was needed only one more morning, as things began to be organised, and as I hung out the washing on the second morning — mostly baby's nappies — I was aware of a formidable woman with a suitcase advancing purposefully up the path. "I am the sister come to take over," she announced, and a flood of relief washed over me. "I am certainly glad to see you," I said. "Washing is not really my thing." She looked at me disparagingly. "Yes," she commented, "I can see that. Some of those nappies could do with a longer boil." Feeling like a tweeny found out by the housekeeper in slovenly work, I pulled down my sleeves, and pedalled home as fast as possible.

The third occasion where the residuary legatee had to be brought in to cope with a crisis where masters were concerned was not physically taxing, but much more alarming. The academic side of school life had, of course, nothing whatsoever to do with me, but there was one occasion when it seemed it had to. The history department at Adams Grammar School was run by an elderly Lancastrian, who was head of the department and a bright younger man who had been appointed by Robert. During one summer term, the head of the department became seriously ill, and it became apparent that he could not return that term, if at all. The junior man took on all he possibly could, and the classes of those actually taking their GCSE and A-level exams that year were certainly covered. A supply teacher was sought to cover the rest of the history teaching for that term, until a permanent man could be appointed for next term. This solved most of the problems, but there was still one for which no solution could be found. The lower sixth were in the middle of a course on 19th-century European history, but the junior master simply had not the time to fit this into his schedule, and the supply teacher maintained he had not the competence to teach that particular period.

What then happened was that one morning as I was peacefully planning next week's menus, Robert suddenly swept into the house, told me of the situation, and concluded, "I am afraid I shall have to ask you to do it." I protested that it was now over twelve years since I had taught, and furthermore, I had never studied that particular period of European history. But Robert swept my protestations aside in a lordly manner. "What nonsense," he said. "You have studied history at university, and you have taught sixth form boys at Lowestoft. And if you don't know much about this particular period you have time to read it up — you need not start till next week — and as for saying you have not taught for over twelve years, you know perfectly well that if you can teach (and you know you can) you can always teach." And with that he swept swiftly and majestically out.

To say I was petrified was an understatement. Young Mr Mottershaw, the junior history master, duly arrived to bring me the necessary books, to fill me in with details of how far the boys had got in the syllabus, and to wish me luck. He also assured me they were a very pleasant bunch of boys. But that was not what was worrying me. I was frightened of letting everyone down, I was sure I would make a fool of myself, and, further, I was very much aware that my teaching methods were very different from those of the senior master. I remembered only too well passing outside a room where he had been teaching and hearing his very distinctive voice saying to the class he had been teaching, "When parliament returned, comma, they found a very different sort of situation, comma, etc.", so that it was perfectly obvious that even at sixth form level he was actually expecting the boys to take down his notes at his dictation. That was certainly not my method of teaching, and if the boys expected this from me, they were in for a shock.

I spent the weekend feverishly studying the period and getting some teaching notes together — in between supervising boys' meals, entertaining the boarding masters to dinner on Saturday, as was our custom, and looking after the preacher on Sunday. I was also spending quite a time looking after the children as Anne always had Saturday afternoon and evening off.

However I felt pretty prepared on Monday morning that I knew at least enough to get through my first lesson, and looked forward — perhaps that is not quite the right word — to welcoming my new class into my dining-room where I was to teach them, on Monday afternoon. There were only eight of them, so they fitted quite well round my large dining-table. We spent a few minutes going over just how far they had got, but when I said, "Right — we'll go on from there", I was alarmed, if not surprised, to see them all open their notebooks, raise their pens, and look expectantly at me. "Now, why are you clutching you pens?" I asked — as if I did not know. "I have not said anything yet. First let us get some facts together and assess what is really relevant, the facts in fact you must remember, and after that I will give you time to make your own notes about them." "Oh, but our old history master always likes us to take down his notes at his dictation," volunteered one brave soul. "Sorry," I said, "with me you will have to get used to being treated like members of the sixth form, not members of the third form, and I can assure you that if you have to think what you are going to write, rather than take down someone else's thoughts, you will remember it better, as it will be part of you." Six of the class looked resigned and put down their pens, but I noticed with amusement the other two continued to hang onto theirs, and I had a strong suspicion that they would still try to take down what I said as I went along. What was interesting was that when they came to do their first essays for me, my two bolshies had simply assembled a heap of accurate facts,

194

while those who had had to think before they wrote their notes had actually drawn some conclusions from them. This gave me the opportunity at the next lesson to launch into one of my favourite soapbox harangues — namely that up to GCSE you are on the whole merely expected to assimilate facts; by the time you reach the sixth form, you are expected to draw your own conclusions from the facts you have and "build" something on them, and understand their wider relevance. For the first part of the term we struggled a bit, but gradually they all got used to me and my methods and I could have cheered when, near the end of term, one of my ex-bolshies said generously, without any prompting, that he was actually convinced that my method of teaching really did make the subject more interesting.

When we said goodbye at the end of term they all said most graciously that they did hope I would be taking them on for their final year. That was nice of them but of course by now Robert had appointed a new history master for next term. So I gave them up with a certain amount of relief, in view of my other commitments — tinged with a tiny bit of regret.

No other crises where I was suddenly called on to find a solution were nearly as important as the teaching one, but two very different odd crises are indelibly fixed in my mind. The first, curiously, concerned a cat. Where it came from no-one knew but one autumn term at Newport we all became aware of a very unpleasant scrawny, mangy, wild cat lurking about the grounds, and, worryingly, drawing nearer and nearer to the school kitchen, no doubt drawn by the warmth and cooking smells. Daytime was not a problem as even with the kitchen door open Mrs Whittle and her broom were an excellent deterrent — she had indeed scored a number of direct "hits". But night-time was more difficult as the caretaker used to come in to make up the boilers and the cat, with all the artfulness of its kind, slipped in behind him and waited until he had gone. Even though nothing was uncovered, the smell in the kitchen in the morning was extremely offensive. It so happened that one night Robert, who had been working late in his school study, came through the kitchen on his way back to the house, and became aware of that singularly pungent and unpleasant smell, and coming into the house simply said, "You will have to do something about that cat — tomorrow".

This was easier said than done, but in the morning I gathered all the resources I could assemble with the object of catching the cat so that we could have it put down. As luck would have it, as we discussed tactics, there was a "sighting" and as the forces advanced the cat streaked past us into the kitchen. For a moment we thought victory was ours as we appeared to have him cornered, but as George Turner the gardener was opening the sack to put him in, the cat again shot past us and upstairs into the school main hall, where it took refuge through a hole in the space under the dais at the far end of the hall. Before anyone could stop him, Tom the gardener's boy, fired by the chase, went in after him, and to my horror there followed several minutes filled with piercing screams and yowlings, until, to my great relief Tom emerged horribly scratched but triumphantly holding the cat in a vice-like grip. In a matter of minutes, the men had the cat safely tied in the sack and off to the vet in the firm custody of George Turner, while I, thoroughly worried by those scratches, took Tom to the out-patients at the local hospital. We all thought that was the end of the story, but not so. That very night Robert, coming through the kitchen again, late at night, smelled that unmistakable smell, and coming into the house announced in some surprise, "I thought you said you had got rid of that cat." So, next morning, after I had taken the children to school I went to see the vet, and in a voice of doom asked what had happened to the body of the cat as there seemed to have been a reincarnation. The vet prevaricated for a moment and then came clean. "The cat was very wild you know," he said (as if I did not know), "and when I opened the sack it was away before I could catch it," adding, "If you can catch it again of course I will not charge to put him down." "Yes," I said and turned back to school to regather my forces. Ultimately the story had a happy ending. The cat had met his match in the redoubtable Tom, who, when he heard the news arrived with a sort of colossal butterfly-net he had made, and that very afternoon spotted his prey hovering in a corner. Starting off at a pace which would not shame an Olympic runner Tom managed to enmesh his foe, who was swearing horribly in cat language, and again George made the trip to the vet. But this time, as he informed me, he told the vet he was going to sit in the waiting-room until he saw the corpse. "And I did," he reported with grim satisfaction.

The story has a rather amusing tail-piece. Next door to the vet's surgery, the vet's wife ran a small antique shop, and as I passed a few days later she called me in. "I know you have been interested in finding the odd local print," she said, "and I have just come on one of 'The Coming of Age of Lord John Pemberton in Newport Market Place'. It is a nice print." "How much?" I asked. "Oh, I would like you to have it as a gift," she said. "You do so much for the town." We still have that rather charming print, known needless to say in the family as "The Cat".

Finally I shall not easily forget a crisis of a very different kind I was called on to cope with once when Robert was actually away during the summer holidays, visiting his mother. I was having an astonishingly peaceful morning actually sitting down reading the paper after breakfast, when Richard, then aged four, wandered in from the school grounds where he had been happily riding his tricycle, remarking conversationally, "I can't get right down the drive this morning — there is a big lorry in the way taking away all those bricks and things they were going to build the new classroom with" — and with that he disappeared. I thought to myself, "That's odd — why take the bricks away?" — and then the penny dropped. I rapidly went through to the kitchen where Mary was cleaning out cupboards and asked her, "What was the name of the local builder you were telling me about who, according to last night's paper, had gone bankrupt?" She told me

198

again and I suddenly realised that was the name of the firm who were supposed to be building our new classroom block. Obviously there was something very wrong here, as, though I do not know much about the law, I was pretty sure that if a builder went bankrupt neither he nor his creditors should move building materials without a court order. In Robert's absence I rang up the old solicitor who acted as clerk to the governors and explained what was going on. "Oh, no-one must move a thing," said the old man at once. "You must go and stop them." This seemed rather a tall order, however throwing on a coat, and wishing I was twenty years older (I was in my early thirties at the time) I advanced down the drive to find the lorry now almost fully loaded with bricks and sand and various pieces of equipment. Two tough-looking labourers were working very much faster than I would have thought usual, and looked up belligerently as I approached. "I am sorry," I said, "but I am afraid you will have to put all that back again." "Who says?" demanded the tougher looking of the two. "We are doing our boss's orders." "Then I am afraid your boss does not realise his legal position," I said as firmly as I could. "I have just been on to our solicitors and they tell me that in view of his present troubles everything must stay exactly where it is." "And who may you be?" demanded the other large man looking down at me from the top of the lorry. "I am the headmaster's wife," I replied, drawing myself up to my full five foot three inches, and adding with sudden inspiration, "My husband is busy at the moment, but I am very happy to ask the solicitor

199

to come round and explain the situation more clearly to you." He looked at me with loathing. "O.K. Jack, chuck it all out again — bloody fuss." And with that they tipped the whole lot out again in an untidy mass all over the drive and drove off.

I was not too popular with our depleted groundstaff who all had to be summoned to move the stuff off the drive. However Robert, when he returned, was very pleased with me and as for Richard he was delighted to be given the opportunity to spend a blissful day wheeling sand about in his little barrow.

When some days later I happened to run into the builder himself in the street I wondered whether I was in for an unpleasant confrontation, but not so. He was a cheerful rogue who did not bear malice, and merely said, looking at me thoughtfully, "Well, I have to say there aren't many as would stand up to Ted and Jack." I could hardly believe my ears.

CHAPTER THIRTEEN

Postscript

Eventually, after 23 years as a headmaster, Robert retired and was delighted to be offered the post of deputy secretary to the Headmasters' Conference, which he thoroughly enjoyed and did with distinction. That of course meant us moving to London, and as I realised my back-up services were now redundant, I foresaw a rather dreary six years with nothing positive to do. I am not good at inaction, and however much my friends commented how lucky I was to be able now to see so many splendid exhibitions, I was not comforted. I therefore decided I must get some sort of a job — despite my children's aghast comments, "At your age mother?" I realised that as I had not done a "proper" job since my mid-twenties it might be difficult to find something, but reasoned, quite correctly, that provided you did not mind particularly what you did (within reason) you would always find something, and I began to look at the "Situations Vacant" columns of *The Times*. Eventually I found one which sounded just like me. It was inserted by an organisation called the Music Trades Association, and what they said they wanted was a "dogsbody". I was interviewed by a young woman to whom I will always be grateful, as she was prepared to take into her office someone with practically no office skills. Some of my friends were slightly shocked. "A dogsbody, Jean — surely you can get something better than that?" But paradoxically Michael McCrum who was headmaster of Eton at the time understood perfectly. He roared with laughter and exclaimed, "Of course you will be the perfect choice — that is what every headmaster's wife is, if she is worth her salt — a dogsbody prepared to cope at all times with whatever comes up." And he added shrewdly, "Once you have a job, whatever it is, you will find it much easier to move on in time to something perhaps more suitable — but you must start somewhere."

And so it happened. I learned my office skills and improved my typing, and did whatever I was called upon to do by the nice young woman who had had enough faith in me to employ me — doing everything from getting the coffee (though I admit it came as a mild but no doubt salutary surprise to be told by the then head of Virgin Records, "Just go and get me a cup of coffee, love") to helping to run a quite prestigious conference at a smart hotel in Stratford. When however Adrienne Rutter my employer left to get married, I thought it might be nice to have a change and worked for a short time in the offices of Stella Fisher the employment ggent, helping in the temps department, and again I rather enjoyed trying to "match" the right sort of young woman to the right employer. However what I did not enjoy was the considerable pressure on us every Friday to make sure all our clients had someone really suitable, and at those times the temperature in the office rose alarmingly. And when I was then asked to work Saturday mornings, which was the time when we always went home to the peace and quiet of Malvern for the weekend, I decided enough was enough. So I looked for calmer waters and got a job in an organisation called Completion Security which dealt with film finance. I went for this particular job as the hours were what I wanted and also its offices were situated in a particularly nice part of London, Albemarle Street, which certainly compared favourably with the environment of my first office which was in Denmark Street.

However after a time I had to admit I found the calmer waters really too calm, and I was getting bored, so when Robert told me there was a job going at ISIS, the Independent Schools Information Service, I applied at once and was delighted to get the job. And if the offices left a certain amount to be desired — at that point they were very cramped — the work was full of interest and what was more I knew something about schools. One of the things I enjoyed most was acting as adviser to parents who wanted help in finding the right school for their son or daughter. Moreover Tim Devlin, who was my boss, absolutely agreed with me that if I was going to advise wisely, I must know as much as possible about the schools I was suggesting. So with his full agreement I spent many happy days visiting schools, particularly the ones which offered something special like help with learning difficulties. That was fun, and I remember so clearly knowing within ten minutes of my arrival at a school whether I was going to like it or not. And I much enjoyed meeting all sorts and conditions of prospective parents — I have a particularly amusing memory of advising an African chieftain, who arrived in full regalia and who had, I soon realised, a highly intelligent daughter. (I also remember his wife being obviously shocked that I did not stand during the interview — "we always stand in his presence," she murmured to me — but fortunately he did not seem to mind.)

But even this, my final job, suddenly developed echoes of the past. When I had first joined ISIS, an organisation known as the Educational Grants Advisory Service had been run by an old colonel in Bedford Square, and from time to time I had been most grateful to him for his advice when parents had a problem. However one day he had a stroke, and it became obvious he was not coming back, and there did not seem anyone capable of taking on his work. I discussed the situation with Tim Devlin. "I keep getting asked by anxious parents where they could possibly find some charitable funding in a crisis," I said. "I suppose it is really up to ISIS to try and find some answers." He looked appalled. "We cannot possibly afford to employ anyone else in the office," he said, "and anyway no-one has the time." Then an all too familiar expression, which I had seen so often on Robert's face, came over his. "Of course, you are really the person most qualified to do it with your knowledge of parents and schools," he said, "but I am afraid I can't pay you any more." I happily did that job of advising parents where they might find charitable help for the next 14 years, taking it with me to Malvern when Robert finally retired.

Plus ça change, plus la même chose.

Also available in ISIS Large Print:

Homing

Alistair Moffat

Alistair Moffat's beautiful memoir recreates his childhood landscape.

"What is important is the chatty and charming way Moffat makes our own cultural past accessible to us."
Independent on Sunday

Alistair Moffat grew up in Kelso, in the Scottish Border country. After the deaths of his grandmother, Bina, and his father, he realised that both had conspired to keep hidden what they saw as a shaming family secret. In *Homing* he vividly recreates his own working-class childhood in Kelso — a lost world of terraced council houses, of local grocery vans and French onion-sellers, and Dan Dare, Digby and Jack Brabham. But his gradual uncovering of Bina's story will finally explain why she, his father and others in the small community of Kelso conspired to keep the family secret.

ISBN 0-7531-9956-4 (hb)
ISBN 0-7531-9957-2 (pb)

I Married Joan

Joan Park

"What kind of a wife do you think Joan would make?" This was the start of the marriage between Joan, a teacher from Liverpool, and Alex Park, eleven years her senior and from Glasgow. Married in 1953, Joan moved to Glasgow and into a very different world from the one she had known, for Alex expected a wife who stayed at home, brought up the children and kept a good house. She, an experienced teacher, wished to continue her career.

Joan Park's account of her marriage, as seen through her husband's eyes, is humorous and encouraging, a wonderful glimpse into the hardships of the immediate post-war years through the changes of the 1960s and 1970s to the present.

ISBN 0-7531-9988-2 **(hb)**
ISBN 0-7531-9989-0 **(pb)**